WEDDING
Etiquette
for DIVORCED
FAMILIES

tasteful advice
for planning a beautiful wedding

martha a. woodham

Contemporary Books

Chicago   New York   San Francisco   Lisbon   London   Madrid   Mexico City
Milan   New Delhi   San Juan   Seoul   Singapore   Sydney   Toronto

Library of Congress Cataloging-in-Publication Data

Woodham, Martha A.
    Wedding Etiquette for Divorced Families / Martha A. Woodham.
       p.   cm.
    Includes index.
    ISBN 0-8092-9710-8
    1. Wedding etiquette.   I. Title.

  BJ2051 .W56   2001
  395.2'2—dc21   2001023517

Contemporary Books

A Division of The McGraw·Hill Companies

2 3 4 5 6 7 8 9 0   AGM/AGM   0 9 8 7 6 5 4 3 2

ISBN 0-8092-9710-8

This book was set in Bembo
Printed and bound by Quebecor Martinsburg

Cover design by Christina Bijak and Monica Baziuk
Cover photograph copyright © Tatsuo Matai & Miki Hayakawa/Photonica
Interior design by Susan H. Hartman

McGraw-Hill books are available at special quantity discounts to use as premiums and sales promotions, or for use in corporate training programs. For more information, please write to the Director of Special Sales, Professional Publishing, McGraw-Hill, Two Penn Plaza, New York, NY 10121-2298. Or contact your local bookstore.

This book is printed on acid-free paper.

To the men and women whose daily commitment to each other
and to their families inspires us all.

Contents

Introduction: How to Use This Book

*W*hat's the biggest problem with getting married today? That ugly "D" word, *divorce*.

Most contemporary families have been touched by divorce, which can create problems that etiquette mavens Amy Vanderbilt and Emily Post never contemplated in the days before no-fault divorces and prenuptial agreements. If you are reading this book, there's a good chance you and your fiancé fit this demographic picture. The statistics are staggering. Fifty percent of marriages in the United States today end in divorce. Factor in your parents and grandparents, and there's an even better chance that divorce is involved in your wedding.

Those past marital splits can haunt an engaged couple about to travel down the aisle together, whether the divorce was his, hers, their parents', or even their grandparents'. Planning a wedding gets complicated when the bride has to decide whether she will be "improper" if she wears a white gown and veil at her second wedding. If children—his or hers—should take part in the ceremony. If newly divorced Mom and Dad can be civil to each other instead of feuding, or if Grandma and her latest husband will consent to sharing a seat with Grandpa and his new wife. Divorce, no matter whose it was, can poison what should be a joyful occasion.

For the past thirteen years, I have been an etiquette columnist, answering questions from brides and grooms on how to handle uncomfortable situations that evolve during their wedding planning. I receive questions from couples all over the country and have included many of their letters in this book so that their experiences can help guide you. Sadly, many of the questions concern divorce. Couples want to know how to plan a wedding when the person who is divorced is

1. the bride,
2. the groom,
3. their parents, or
4. all of the above.

Many traditional etiquette books still ignore divorce as a fact of life—despite the fact that approximately 35 percent of the women and men marrying today are marching down the aisle for the second, third, or even fourth time.

So what's a modern couple to do? For decades, the stigma against divorce meant remarriage was done quietly, without the frills of a first marriage. And today, although remarriage has become much more accepted, many people don't want to admit they are marrying for the third or fourth time. Couples don't want to be improper, yet they do want to celebrate their commitment to each other. It may not be "'til death do us part," but couples want to savor this shining moment with taste and grace. And they should.

No matter how divorce has touched your life, this book is your reference guide to what's proper and gracious. Topics, from attire to budgeting to

> "You can get through life with bad manners, but it's easier with good manners."
> —*Lillian Gish*

wedding style, are organized alphabetically, so you won't have to hunt for the information you need. Puzzled over wording invitations when your parents are divorced? Look up Invitations. Wondering if your children should be in your wedding party? You'll find answers under Attendants and Children. Begin with the Planning Calendar, which follows, where you will find a countdown to your wedding day. This checklist of tasks and deadlines for their completion will help keep you focused and your planning on track in the months and weeks before the big day.

> ∞ "There is no more lovely, friendly, and charming relationship, communion, or company than a good marriage."
> —*Martin Luther*

Planning a wedding is never stress-free, but this book can make things easier for you by answering your trickiest questions, whether it's how to get everyone's name on the wedding invitations or how to form a receiving line with four sets of parents. And, most importantly, you'll learn that divorce should never be a barrier to a joyous wedding day.

PLANNING CALENDAR

This is a basic calendar to help keep you organized, whether you are planning your first wedding or your second. If you do not have the luxury of twelve months to plan your wedding, set priorities. Wedding consultant Susan Pando of Creative Events in Atlanta says couples should immediately reserve their wedding and reception site, photographer, and band because the best ones are booked far in advance.

Many couples marrying for the second time opt for much smaller, more informal weddings than the first time around, so feel free to adjust this checklist to suit your needs. Do not think that just because something is on this list that you must make it part of your wedding plans. After all, monogrammed napkins are not for everyone.

B: Bride's job
G: Groom's job

B or G: It doesn't matter who handles these arrangements, but
someone must be in charge.

B & G: You've got to work together on this.

Twelve Months Ahead or ASAP

B & G: Select a date.

B & G: Begin compiling your guest list.

B & G: Decide how many people will be invited.

B & G: Set a budget. Agree on how expenses will be shared.

B & G: If you want to use a bridal consultant, find one you like and
trust.

B & G: Find a place to get married. Reserve it.

B & G: Confer with your clergy person on the date.

B & G: Pick a site for the reception. Reserve it.

B & G: Hire a caterer, if necessary.

B & G: If you want a popular band for the reception, book it.

B or G: Find a wedding photographer (if needed). Hire her.

B & G: Talk to your parents about their guest list. Tell them how
many people they can invite and give them a deadline.

B or G: Start a card or computer file of your guests, their mailing
and E-mail addresses, and their phone numbers. Include
space to record acceptances and regrets as well as gifts and
whether thank-you notes have been sent.

B: Begin shopping for the wedding gown and for the
attendants' attire.

B & G: Plan your wedding trip.

Six Months Ahead

B: Find the bridal outfit. Set up a fittings schedule and a
delivery date. If the bride is wearing an heirloom gown,
check on any repairs or alterations the dress may need.

B: Select the bridesmaids' attire. Don't forget to set up a
fittings schedule and a delivery date.

B or G: Meet with your florist to choose the flowers.

B or G: Meet with your caterer to select a menu.

B or G: Find a wedding videographer (if needed). Book her.

B & G: Select your wedding attendants.

Three Months Ahead

B & G: Order stationery: invitations and announcements (if needed), personal stationery, thank-you notes, place cards, monogrammed napkins (not required). Be sure to ask for proofs so you can check for errors.

B: Choose favors for reception (if needed).

B & G: Select a guest book.

B: Schedule an appointment for the bridal portrait, if desired.

B & G: Meet with the organist or musicians to select music for the ceremony (if appropriate).

B: Schedule bridesmaids' fittings.

B & G: Decide upon the groom's attire and that of his attendants. Shop for it or rent it (as needed).

B & G: Shop for attendants' gifts.

B or G: Order your wedding cake if your caterer does not provide it.

B or G: Order any rental equipment necessary for the reception: chairs, tables, linens, candelabra, and so forth.

B & G: Confer with whoever will be hosting the rehearsal dinner (usually the groom's parents) about the party: where it will be held, who is invited, menu, and so forth.

B & G: Begin making transportation and accommodation plans for your family and out-of-town guests.

B & G: Book hotel rooms for guests (if needed).

Two Months Ahead

B & G: Meet with the minister and schedule premarital counseling. Tell him or her now if you want changes in the ceremony or wish to write your own vows.

B & G: Address and stamp invitations. At post office, ask that your invitations be "hand canceled." Postal machines often damage invitations.

B & G: Begin keeping your gift record and writing your thank-you notes as gifts arrive. Thank-you notes should be sent within two weeks of receiving a gift.

B & G: Find out what medical tests, if any, are required for a marriage license.

B & G: Make your personal appointments: legal, insurance, medical, and so forth.

B: Book stylist for hair, nails, and makeup.

B & G: Decide where to live after the wedding.

B & G: Send change of address cards to financial institutions, magazines, insurance companies, and so forth.

Six Weeks Ahead

B or G: Mail your invitations.

B & G: Buy and engrave your wedding rings.

Four Weeks Ahead

B or G: Double check with the professionals you've hired: caterer, florist, stylist, musicians, reception-site manager, photographer, and videographer.

B & G: Schedule your wedding rehearsal (if needed). Notify your attendants.

B: Make sure the bride has her wedding outfit accessories.

B & G: Finalize the guest list for the rehearsal dinner.

B & G: Buy attendants' gifts if you have not done so.

B & G: Continue writing those thank-you notes!

Two Weeks Ahead

B & G: Have final fittings of all wedding attire. Bride, request that your gown be ironed or steamed the day before the wedding, when you will pick it up.

B or G: Have final consultation with the professionals you've hired: caterer, florist, stylist, musicians, reception-site manager, photographer, and videographer.

B & G: Plan seating arrangements if needed.

B or G: Consult with the host and hostess of the rehearsal dinner to make sure the invitations have been mailed.

B or G: Send wedding announcements to newspapers.

G: Get marriage license.

B & G: Confirm your honeymoon reservations. Make sure you have all the necessary papers: tickets, passports, traveler's checks, and so forth.

B & G: Keep writing those thank-you notes!

One Week Ahead

G: Pick up the wedding outfits.

B or G: Confirm the guest count. Inform the caterer and the reception-site manager.

B or G: Touch base with the professionals you've hired: caterer, musicians, photographer, florist, reception-site manager, videographer, and stylist. Give them a contact and number to call in case of emergencies

∞ "Though marriage is intimate and personal, it also has an inherently public side. Marriage is what lovers do when they want to bring their relationship out of the realm of personal emotions and make it a social fact, visible to and recognized not only by the couple, but also by friends, family, church, government, and the rest of society. Good marriages are made, not born, and they are most likely to be made in a society that understands and values marriage as a shared aspiration and a key social institution, not just a private affair of the heart."

—*The Marriage Movement*

B & G: Pack for your wedding trip.

B & G: Don't forget those thank-you notes!

Day Before the Wedding

B: Pick up freshly ironed gown.

Day of the Wedding

B & G: You're prepared, so relax and enjoy it!

Attendants

Selecting Your Wedding Party

So many best friends . . . so little space! Selecting who will be in the wedding party is not an easy task. Being a bridesmaid or a groomsman carries certain responsibilities, and brides and grooms need to make sure that the people they select can handle the job. To their dismay, many brides find that friends they were counting on to help with wedding duties are no-shows who can't be trusted. Still other "friends" do nothing but complain, which is the last thing a nervous bride needs.

Some couples find themselves feeling pressured by friends or family who want to be in the wedding. The couples end up feeling guilty when they can't accommodate these extras or—worse—give in and include them, only to regret it later when the wedding budget is blown.

Focus on family, and the rest will fall into place. All too often brides, especially younger brides, want to ask their best pals to be bridesmaids instead of asking sisters and cousins. These brides forget that a wedding is a family affair. In the years to come, the friend she whispered secrets to in first-period algebra probably will be out of her life, but she sees her sister-in-law every Thanksgiving. Her fiancé's sister, now a stranger, could be her best friend some day. A wedding is the time to build those relationships.

The same logic applies to their parents' children from another marriage. If there are stepsiblings or half-siblings, the gracious couple will find a place for them in the wedding party. The generous gesture will be appreciated.

A bride with an abundance of friends often falls into another trap, one of spontaneity. In the excitement of telling friends about her engagement, she impulsively asks each and every one to be a bridesmaid. When reality sets in, she finds that she will have a cast of thousands at the altar. Then she faces the embarrassing situation of having to inform friends that she made a mistake and would like them to pour punch instead.

HOW TO SELECT YOUR WEDDING PARTY

Selecting attendants should not be done impulsively, but rather with the same thought and care that goes into the rest of the wedding planning. These guidelines will help you avoid regretting your choices.

This is between the two of you. Discuss your wedding party and make sure you are both comfortable with each other's selections *before* you start asking people to be in the wedding. The bride may find out that her fiancé is uncomfortable around a friend of hers who made a pass at him, or he may learn that his cousin gives his bride the creeps.

Start with siblings. A wedding is the joining of two families, and being in the wedding party is a wonderful way for the bride's and groom's siblings to get to know one another. The bride who whines "But I'm not *close* to his sister" is an insensitive ninny who is creating in-law problems. Make it a family affair.

A wedding party is not an equal-opportunity employer. So what if the bride has four bridesmaids and the groom five groomsmen? The Great Etiquette God is not going to come down from the sky and smite them because their wedding party is not symmetrical. A creative altar arrangement of the wedding personnel should take care of this little problem. For example, instead of having the women on one side of the church and the men on the other, position both sexes on each side, with the women standing between and just in front of the men. The extra man stands on the groom's side. During the recessional, he either exits with the last bridesmaid and groomsman or he walks out alone.

Just say "no" to pushy friends who want to be in the wedding. A nice excuse—"I'm sorry, you are a good friend, and I know you will under-stand when we say our budget/space/wedding size is limited"—soothes hurt feelings.

Remember: not everyone in the wedding party has to be younger than the bride and groom. It's perfectly fine to ask older friends or treasured rel-atives to be attendants in the wedding. They would consider it an honor.

A bride or groom who can't choose between two best friends or who has more than one sibling need not play favorites. Ask *both* best friends to be honor attendants and divvy up the duties between them. One bride, who had three sisters, asked her best friend to be the maid of honor so she wouldn't have to choose between her sisters.

A bride writes: My fiancé's sister "expects" to be in our wedding. She is only a year older than I am, but we do not know each other that well except that I am engaged to her brother. We do not get along and are as opposite as night and day. She has asked on two occasions if she was going to be in my wedding, once coming right out and saying, "Am I going to be in the wedding or in the pew?" Not knowing what to say, I told her I wasn't sure what I wanted her to do yet. Please tell me how I can handle this situation. I have already chosen my bridesmaids, who are my dearest high school friends and have several other friends who will be handling the guest register and other tasks. There is really no place for her, and I simply do not feel that I should have her in my wedding simply because she is my fiancé's sister. He has told me that he will stand behind whatever decision I make. (Please keep in mind that she is an unwed mother.) —BRIDAL DILEMMA

> If I could change anything about my wedding, I would ask my fiancé's sister to be a bridesmaid. I created a rift between my mother-in-law and me that I don't think will ever truly heal. And I felt like such an ungracious jerk when his sister asked me to be in her wedding two years later. ∝

DEAR DILEMMA: Sorry, but you won't get any help from me about shutting this girl out of your wedding. And her marital status has nothing to do with it. I happen to believe that not asking a fiancé's siblings to be in the wedding party is extremely shortsighted and very hurtful.

Traditionally, family is included in the wedding party. After the wedding, his sister will be *your* sister, too, whether you are "close" to her or not. Your relationship with your sister-in-law will last for decades, and you are not starting it off on a good note. Leaving her out of the wedding will create a hurt that will linger and will not be easy to forget and may last longer than some of your "close" high school friendships will.

A word to the wise: leaving her out makes you look bad. She may be the one who is difficult and selfish, but that is not how it will look to his family's friends and relations. Your wedding is "your" day, but that doesn't give you the right to be a bully. The gracious bride is always considerate and thinks of others. Make room for your fiancé's sister and quit wasting energy worrying about it.

A bride writes: I have asked my half-sister to be my maid of honor, although I would have preferred my cousin. We are closer, but I thought she could not afford the attire. Now I find out that she has the funds. I want her, but I don't want to hurt my half-sister's feelings. I know this situation is my fault, but I don't know how to get out of it. —FEELING GUILTY

DEAR GUILTY: Your signature answered your question for you. You feel guilty because you know that dumping your half-sister *would* hurt her feelings, yet you selfishly hope I will get you off the hook. Well, I won't. It would be rude for you to uninvite your half-sister to be your maid of honor. Ask your cousin to be a bridesmaid instead.

> "In Hollywood all marriages are happy. It's trying to live together afterwards that causes all the problems."
> —*Shelley Winters*

A bride writes: My mom and I have been very close, more like best friends. I would really like for her to be more a part of the ceremony. Seating her in the front of the church doesn't seem to be enough, but I don't think she would be comfortable standing up as my maid of honor. —MOM'S PAL

DEAR PAL: Of course, you may ask your mother to be your matron of honor, but she has enough to do as mother of the bride. The very best way to honor your mother takes place out of the church: seeing you make a success of your marriage.

THE ATTENDANTS IN SECOND WEDDINGS

Traditionally, couples marrying for the second (or third) time had only one attendant each. Divorce was so taboo that it was considered gauche to draw attention to one's self. Celebrities such as Elizabeth Taylor and

Zsa Zsa Gabor once may have scandalized the American public with their multiple trips down the aisle, but even these matrimony marathoners usually had just one attendant each time.

As divorce became the American way of life, the rules on second weddings have relaxed, and no one thinks twice about second-time brides having several attendants, particularly if the groom has never been married.

This is the time to rely on family and include your children *if* they are happy about the person you are marrying. Some families even turn the wedding into a celebration of the new family with the new brothers and sisters exchanging rings or necklaces as well. Of course, this is *not* recommended if you are the person who broke up their parents' marriage.

"How Many Bridesmaids and Groomsmen Do We Need?"

For the first wedding: five or six each is the average, but usually one groomsman is needed for every fifty guests in order to escort guests to their seats.

For second weddings: one or two each will suffice.

"Who Will Be Our Honor Attendants?"

The honor attendants usually are the bride's sisters, dearest friends, or, in a second marriage, her older children. The best man may be the groom's father, brother, close relative, friend, or, in a second marriage, his older children.

"What About Our Children?"

In a second marriage, the couple's children can participate as bridesmaids, groomsmen, flower girls, or ring bearers. However, they usually are not honor attendants unless they are older.

A bride writes: This is my second wedding, and I have three children, twin girls age seven, and a boy, nine. I would like for my children to stand with us when we say our vows. Will I need anyone else as a witness or to stand with us as we are married? I would like to wear a tea-length pink dress and dress the twins in pink or white. What do my fiancé and son wear to go with what we are wearing? Tuxedos? —CONFUSED BUT HAPPY

If I could change anything about my wedding, I would be more selective about the person I asked to be my matron of honor. She was not supportive, which created extra stress.

∞

DEAR CONFUSED: Having your children as your attendants is a great way to get your new family started. You will need an adult to witness the wedding license, but that person does not have to be in the wedding party.

Your fiancé and son would wear suits, which will make them much happier than having to dress up in penguin suits.

A bride writes: My fiancé has a twenty-four-year-old daughter and a sixteen-year-old son. I have an eighteen-year-old son. Our children are thrilled with our decision to get married and become a family. Could we have them as attendants? Who stands where? Could my son serve as my "mister of honor"?
—MOTHER AND THE BRIDE

DEAR MOM: By all means have your kids in the wedding, in whatever configurations you choose. But, please, don't saddle anyone with the title of "mister of honor." Simply call your children your "attendants."

At the altar, your fiancé's children may stand on his side and your son on yours. You may even have your son escort you down the aisle, if you wish.

A bride writes: I have chosen my sister as my maid of honor and my fiancé's sister as a bridesmaid. My fiancé has chosen his best man and is pondering whom to ask to be a groomsman. He has a thirteen-year-old son from a previous marriage. My fiancé's mother and sister think the boy should be the other attendant. I am not altogether at ease with this. I am concerned about the boy's maturity in this situation. Would he be treated as any other member of the wedding party and be seated at the head table? What are some alternative roles he could play? Would his mother have to be invited? —STEPMOTHER BRIDE

DEAR STEPMOM-TO-BE: I think that children from former marriages should always be included in a wedding—if they wish. A wedding is the creation of a new family, and children are very much part of that family. In fact, they can be a main reason second marriages fail.

Here is your chance to act like a real mother and not merely a step-mom more concerned about appearances than with what is truly important: making a thirteen-year-old boy feel loved and wanted at a special moment in his father's life. Nothing is more important than that, especially not who sits where or some rigmarole about the boy's "maturity."

I think the real reason for your anxiety about the boy is actually anxiety about his mom. No, you don't have to invite her.

A bride writes: I have two daughters, ages five and two. I want them to be flower girls, but everyone is mad at me because they want their children or their nieces and nephews in my wedding. What should I do? —IN A QUANDARY

DEAR QUANDARY: I'd get new friends. Anyone who gets "mad" at you because you prefer your children to theirs is not worth worrying about.

THE ATTENDANTS' RESPONSIBILITIES AND DUTIES

A bridesmaid's job primarily is to look her best and flirt with the groomsmen. But the exalted position of attendant—both bridesmaids and groomsmen—does come with certain responsibilities. Bridesmaids and groomsmen must:

- Buy or rent their outfits
- Keep their fitting appointments
- Support the bride and groom and offer to help with various tasks as needed
- Give a gift to the couple either individually or as a group
- Entertain the couple with a shower
- Be on time to the rehearsal and the wedding
- Mingle with the guests at the reception
- Not show up drunk

The Maid of Honor and the Matron of Honor

The bride may have either a maid or a matron or both, if she wishes. The honor attendant:

- Helps compile the guest list and address invitations
- Helps select the bridesmaids' gowns
- Organizes a shower for the bride (or a coed shower for the couple)
- Gives a gift to the couple either individually or with the bridesmaids
- Assists the bride and her mother with last-minute errands
- Helps the bride dress for the wedding
- Collects the bride's personal effects at the wedding site
- Keeps the groom's wedding ring until the officiant asks for it during the service
- Holds the bride's bouquet and adjust her train during the ceremony
- Witnesses the signing of the marriage license
- Stands in the receiving line
- Toasts the couple at the reception

If the bride has two honor attendants, these duties are divided between them. ∞

The Best Man

The groom usually has only one best man, but he may have two if he chooses. The best man:

- Entertains the couple or organizes the bachelor party
- Gives a gift to the couple either individually or with the groomsmen
- Assists the groom and the bride's mother with last-minute errands
- May arrange to have flowers and/or wine waiting for the couple on their wedding night
- Packs the couple's luggage into their car for their getaway
- Helps the groom dress for the wedding
- Drives the groom to the site of the wedding
- Ensures that the groom has the marriage license
- Gives the minister his fee from the groom
- Reminds the groom to remove his gloves as the bride enters
- Holds the bride's ring until the officiant requests it during the ceremony
- Witnesses the signing of the marriage license
- Toasts the couple at the reception
- Dances with the bride, the mothers, and other honored guests
- Assists the couple as they make their getaway

What's the Difference Between a Groomsman and an Usher?

Not much. Both escort guests to their seats, but only the groomsmen participate in the processional. If more men are necessary to seat guests than the groom wishes to have standing up for him at the altar, then extra men are asked to be ushers.

ARE WE HAVING FUN YET?

Despite women's lib, bachelor parties, where men get drunk and naked women jump out of giant cakes, are not things of the past. Men today often repair to a strip club for the festivities. And it's not unheard of for a bride to be feted in a similar fashion with a male stripper. But not everyone thinks this kind of "fun" is, well, fun. The honor attendants and the best man should confer with the couple before planning such events and follow their wishes.

Usually couples marrying for the second time have outgrown this kind of foolishness.

Brides

Beauty Is Skin Deep

*T*he woman who believes that her wedding will be "my day" gets a rude awakening just after her fiancé slips that diamond on her finger. Everyone, right down to the bride's best friend's next-door neighbor, also has an idea of what the wedding should be—and these notions rarely agree.

"It's *your* day. It's *your* day. It's *your* day." This is the mantra that · runs through books and magazines on wedding planning today. "It's *your* day. It's *your* day. It's *your* day." And it is . . . a bride's wedding day is her day filled with joy and happiness and excitement and love.

Unfortunately, too many brides hear "It's *your* day" as "It's *my* day to do whatever I want and no one can stop me." This bride is the one who will disregard her parents' budget limitations, who refuses to ask her fiancé's siblings to be in the wedding party, who insists upon rewriting wedding tradition to suit herself, who controls the bridesmaids like a dictator, who disregards well-meant suggestions from her in-laws, and heaven knows what else.

Becoming engaged does not give a woman carte blanche to do whatever her little heart desires. Instead, that ring sparkling on her finger should be a reminder that she must be especially attentive to the feelings of those around her. She must never forget that, while she is its glorious center of attention, a wedding is the joining of two families. And as these two families come together, each member brings different expectations of what a wedding should be. Unfortunately, these ideas and expectations sometimes clash.

A wedding is often a woman's formal introduction to the art of compromise. The bride will feel pulled in more directions than Elizabeth Taylor has ex-husbands as she tries to plan a wedding while keeping everyone—mothers, fathers, stepparents, relatives, bridesmaids—happy. And for the family that doesn't get along, watch out!

So how does the gracious bride keep everyone smiling?

> ∞ "In marriage be thou wise. Prefer the person before money, virtue before beauty, the mind before the body; then thou hast a wife, a friend, a companion, a second self."
>
> —*William Penn*

• She is tactful, taking time to listen to everyone's complaints and suggestions, offering compromises where possible. This makes all who are involved feel as if they are vital parts of the wedding.

• She is polite, thanking everyone for all their time and trouble. This lets everyone know how much she cares about them and appreciates their efforts.

• She becomes an expert at compromise. One definition of compromise is "something blending the characteristics of two others." And what else is a wedding but a blending of two to create the new?

• She turns to the ultimate authorities, etiquette books, to resolve disagreements on what is correct. Most people who are sure they are *the* experts on what's proper will back down when there's something in writing from a reliable source.

• She keeps smiling. A happy face and soft tone of voice will frequently diffuse tense situations and avoid confrontations.

These tips have a strange side effect. As the bride focuses on others, she finds that she's happier, too!

Budgets

Planning a Wedding Within Your Means

From the time a woman is a little girl, she dreams of what her wedding will be like. She'll glow as she floats down the aisle on a cloud of white silk, her veil streaming behind her. Perhaps she was secretly influenced by Walt Disney's *Cinderella*, or maybe she's seen videos of the real-life royal wedding of Charles and Diana. And, of course, there are those fabulous photographs in wedding magazines to give her ideas.

But then reality hits. She and her fiancé aren't royalty, and they don't live in castles. They face budgets and stressed-out mothers and maybe a bridesmaid a bit on the chunky side. The couple knows life's not a video, but they want everything to be perfect for just one day, their wedding day.

Whether this is your first marriage or your third, money is always an issue in wedding planning. Too many newly engaged women rush off to the bridal salon to find the dress of their dreams, only to wipe out their budgets. Slow down and set priorities.

What is most important to you about your wedding? What kind of memories do you want of your day? What does "getting married" mean to you?

The gracious bride knows that no matter what her budget, she can have the wedding every woman dreams of—a joyous wedding. Her heart is filled with love—for the man she is about to marry, for her family, and for her friends. She and her groom offer the hospitality that can be afforded. The couple is thrilled that those they hold dear have made the effort to come be with them on their wedding day, to support them at this important junction in life.

The couple knows that dresses and menus and wedding gifts and all the other details we can become so obsessed with don't matter in the long run. What counts are the people. And when the bride and groom replay the day in their minds' video, the memories will be of the happiness on the faces of those who shared their wedding day. And

 ## The Budget Breakdown

This simple breakdown should give you a very rough idea of how your expenses will run. Of course, you will tweak your figures as necessary. For example, if the wedding gown is more important to you than the flowers, plan on spending a little more on the dress and less on the floral arrangements. Plan on spending:

- 50 percent of your budget on the reception
- 10 percent on the gown and bridal accessories
- 10 percent on the flowers
- 10 percent on the music
- 10 percent on the photography and videography
- 10 percent on incidentals

that is where the planning should begin—with the guest list. After all, you will remember the smile on Aunt Susie's face far longer than you will recall whether you served shrimp.

For great advice on cost-saving tips, pick up Sharon Naylor's *1001 Ways to Save Money . . . and Still Have a Dazzling Wedding.* ∞

The bridal couple should decide whom they want to attend. Just family? Close friends, too? A blowout with all Mom and Dad's friends as well?

Now, consider how much money you have to spend. If you are on a limited budget (and who isn't?) and have large families, it stands to reason that, for the money, you can afford to invite more guests to a simple wedding.

A bride writes: We are on a limited budget because we are financing the wedding ourselves. How do we determine whom to invite to the ceremony and whom to the ceremony and reception? —PINCHING PENNIES

DEAR PENNIES: I would like to remind everyone that most people planning a wedding are on a limited budget. Just because your parents are paying for your wedding doesn't mean you have free range with their AmEx card.

Now, whom to invite. Start with your wedding party and spouses and then build: your immediate families; your close friends; your once-removed relatives, such as cousins; your not-so-close friends; and co-workers. I would draw the line at the lady at the dry cleaners or the guy who grooms your dog.

Usually everyone invited to the ceremony is also invited to the reception. Sometimes couples may have a small ceremony with just family and intimate friends that is followed by a larger reception, but the reverse is rarely true. If a lavish reception for the number of people you wish to invite is out of your price range, plan a simpler reception before you start whittling away at your guest list.

A bride writes: The budget for our wedding is a huge concern. My fiancé's parents have considerably more money than my parents do. The guest list consists of 250 to 300 people, and only 57 of them are on the bride's side. We truly want a fabulous reception, but the cost is skyrocketing, even though I have been working hard to cut corners. The budget is edging over the limits set by my parents. How do I approach his family about contributing to the cost of the reception? I don't think that they will offer to help because my parents are good about faking their economic status. And I don't want to embarrass my parents.
—Bridal Bind

Dear Bridal: It may be too late for you, but your sad experience may help other brides. When couples begin planning their weddings, each side should be given a limit on the number of guests to be invited.

Unfortunately, you and your fiancé did not do this, and now you are playing catch up. I suggest that you and your fiancé (a united front is better) discuss this with both sets of parents. You will have to take charge. His parents sound as if they are out of control and your parents have lost the ability to just say "no."

Tell all of them that you are not comfortable with a large wedding and want to downsize. Then do it. Have a small wedding and reception. If his parents wish to honor you with a larger affair after the honeymoon, let them. It is ridiculous to go into debt over a wedding. And it is even sillier to hurt yourself financially trying to "keep up appearances" in front of people you don't even know.

Who Pays for This Wedding?

The answer to who pays for the wedding is easy for first-time brides: dear old Dad. The parents of the groom usually pay for the rehearsal dinner, but the bulk of the wedding expenses traditionally falls on the bride's parents, who act as hosts for this social occasion. But as wedding costs have grown to equal the cost of a small house, many families find it fairer to share costs.

If the bride and groom are older and support themselves, then they should pay the bulk of the expenses, especially if they live together—even if this is the bride's first marriage. If the groom's family falls into the category of Fabulously Wealthy (we're talking megabucks), they may offer to put on the wedding in the grand style to which they have become accustomed.

When the bride's parents are divorced or separated, they are no longer a social unit who wish to entertain their guests together. The issue of who pays for what can become a power struggle. The parent with the best bottom line may try to use paying the bills to dictate family behavior at the wedding. Fathers who have shirked their child-support payments or who now have second families are not always eager to give money to daughters they may rarely see.

When it comes to divorced parents, there is no right way or wrong way to divide costs. Divorced families frequently find the most expedient and equitable means of divvying up the bills is for the mother to pay the ceremony expenses while the father, who usually has more income, picks up the tab for the reception. Often, when faced with negotiating this emotional quagmire, couples simply decide to pay for everything themselves. Each family is different, and the couple must talk candidly with their parents to decide what will work best in their situation.

In the case of a bride's divorce, is it fair to expect Mom and Dad to give their daughter another send-off into the arms of yet another man she will promise to love " 'til death us do part"? No. They've done their duty. The second time around, the financial burden falls on the bride and groom.

A bride writes: Doesn't the groom's family pay for anything? —BUDGETING

If the parents of the bride can afford it, they may choose to pay for the attendants' clothing. ∞

DEAR BUDGETING: Yes, the following list explains what expenses the groom and his family usually pick up. Compared with the bride's family, the groom's family doesn't seem to be financially challenged. But with the mega-expenses of today's weddings, more families are stepping in, checkbooks in hand, to help bear the burden. This is perfectly acceptable. The only rules are that the bride's family cannot *demand* that the groom's family pitch in, and budgeting should be determined up front. No fair surprising the groom's family with the bar bill after the wedding.

For Richer, for Poorer

The following list is the traditional breakdown of expenses for a wedding. It may vary slightly according to the local custom in your area of the country. And, of course, your family and your fiancé's may change it to suit your needs—just be sure everyone knows what's expected.

Expenses of the Bride's Family
- The announcement party, if there is one
- Expenses associated with the ceremony, unless listed otherwise
- The printing of invitations and announcements; mailing expenses
- All reception expenses, including food, liquor, music, and service, unless listed otherwise
- Flowers used for decoration and other arrangements (Please see Flowers.)
- The wedding cake
- Fees for those assisting with the ceremony (organist, consultant, soloist, and so forth)
- Photography and videography

- A gift for the couple
- The bride's attire
- Their own wedding attire and that of their other children
- Parking and security, if needed
- Insurance for wedding gifts
- Accommodations for the bride's attendants

Expenses of the Groom's Family

- A gift for the bride and groom
- The rehearsal dinner and invitations
- Their own travel and hotel expenses
- Their wedding attire
- Any entertaining for the bride and groom, such as a reception to introduce the bride to their friends

The Bride's Expenses

- A gift for the groom
- The groom's ring
- Gifts for her attendants, including a remembrance for the flower girl
- A bridesmaids' party, unless a friend or relative is hosting it
- Wedding guest book
- Personal stationery and thank-you notes

> The parents of the ring bearer and the flower girl pay for their children's clothing.
>
>

The Groom's Expenses

- A gift for the bride
- The engagement and wedding rings
- The honeymoon
- The wedding license
- The officiant's fee
- His wedding attire

- Gifts for his attendants, including a remembrance for the ring bearer
- Gloves and ties, if they are to be worn by his attendants
- Accommodations for out-of-town men in the wedding party
- The bride's bouquet and other arrangements (Please see Flowers.)

The Attendants' Expenses
- Wedding attire
- Travel expenses
- A gift for the couple
- Any entertaining they do for the bride and groom such as showers or a bachelor party

A bride writes: My parents divorced when I was young, and I grew up with a wonderful man for a stepfather. Recently, my natural father has come back into my life, and we have a nice relationship. Now I am planning to get married. Who is responsible for paying for the wedding? —Two Dads

If I could change anything about my wedding, I would have been more disciplined about sticking to my budget. Our wedding ended up costing us about $3,000 more than we had planned.

Dear Dads: Usually the bride's mother (and stepfather) handle the expenses from the wedding ceremony, such as the flowers, the bride's gown, the attendants' gifts, and so forth. The father, usually because he is more able to afford it, pays for the reception. This is not written in stone, and expenses can be adjusted accordingly.

A bride writes: This is my fiancé's first wedding, and he wants a traditional church ceremony (with three attendants each) followed by a reception for about 120 guests. Since this is my second wedding, my parents refuse to pay for it, so my fiancé and I are footing the

bill. But he thinks tradition should be followed to some extent and that my folks should offer to pay for something. Because of this, it seems like my parents feel that this wedding isn't quite as special or good as my first one, which they did pay for. —ONE MORE TIME

DEAR ONE MORE TIME: The tradition concerning second—or more—marriages is a sexist one. It depends only on a woman's former marital status. An oft-divorced man may have several big formal weddings if each fiancé has never been married, but tradition decrees that a bride is limited to one lavish display. After that, everything about the ceremony and reception is toned down, and—perhaps most importantly—the bride's parents are not obligated to pay for any of it.

Your fiancé is wrong to resent your parents' refusal to pay for your second wedding. Not only is it crass to expect someone to pay for something, but your parents already have fulfilled any responsibility to you as far as weddings go. It is not their fault that your first one did not work out.

Their refusal to pay does not mean they don't think this wedding is "as good" as your first one. How "good" and "special" this marriage will be is up to you.

A Word to the Wise

Many couples try to save money by doing everything themselves, from making favors and pew bows to printing the programs. Some brides go to elaborate lengths, gluing thousands of dried rose petals on paper cones to make centerpieces à la Martha Stewart. It's not worth the money you save if you are killing yourself to get everything done. Brides have enough to do without making themselves crazy over finding just the right lace for little sacks of almonds. Get help or forget unnecessary frills.

A stepmother of the bride writes: My stepdaughter is getting married next year. We love her and have always been close. However, since her engagement she has made it clear that she expects her father (my husband) to pay for her whole wedding. Her father and mother have been divorced for seven years, and it has not been amicable. The groom's parents are in the same situation. I have tried to let her know tactfully that the other parents should contribute by dropping hints like "as each parent contributes. . . ." But it seems she and her fiancé expect her father to do it all. Shouldn't a wedding be a shared event when it comes to expenses? My husband has not worked for a year because of his health, which his daughter is very aware of. Initially, my husband did not want to pay for anything because his daughter is almost thirty and has been on her own and living with her fiancé for more than four years. I insisted that we pay a reasonable portion, but we cannot do it all. Emotions are raging— help! —ANXIOUS STEPMOTHER

DEAR ANXIOUS: Traditionally, the bulk of the wedding expenses were paid by the bride's father. This was also in the days when a woman did not leave her father's home until after she married, and parents rarely divorced.

Since your stepdaughter is a "mature" bride—older and wiser— who has been living with her fiancé, the gracious thing for the couple to do is to insist on paying for the wedding. It is not fair for a woman who has been out of her father's home for almost a decade to revert to childhood and demand that dear old Dad pay all the wedding expenses. In addition, your husband's health problems have also affected his income. As a stepmother, you are more than generous to insist that he contribute.

Since graciousness does not seem to be in your stepdaughter's vocabulary, my suggestion is that you and your husband decide how much you can afford to give your stepdaughter for the wedding. Tell her that because of your limited finances, this amount would be the same even if she were living under your roof. It is now up to her to work within that budget or to add to it if she wishes a more elaborate wedding. Realize, of course, that you will have little say-so in the wedding planning.

Do not get involved in negotiations between her and her mother or the fiancé's parents. What they may wish to contribute is their affair. The amounts need not be "equal." And do not offer to pay for certain parts of the wedding, liquor or flowers, for instance. That would be like giving her a blank check.

If I could change anything about my wedding, I would give my future mother-in-law a limit on the number of people on her guest list. Her list alone had more than 150 people! ∝

The Ceremony

The Moment We've All Been Waiting For

*T*his is it. Guests are arriving, and your wedding is about to begin. Thanks to the Great Etiquette God, the bride with divorced parents can go down the aisle knowing her sticky situations have been handled beautifully.

- All of the parents and stepparents have been seated properly. (Please see Seating.)
- The question of who will escort the bride has been answered to everyone's satisfaction. (Please see Escorting the Bride.)
- The attendants are on time and ready to take their places. (Please see Attendants.)
- Everyone is dressed beautifully, with the bride in a sophisticated, sleek dress, and the groom in a dashing suit. (Please see Clothing.)

Ceremony Countdown for First Marriages (Christian)

The following format is commonly used when neither the bride nor the groom has been married. Most weddings follow a similar organization, although it can be tweaked to suit each couple's needs.

1. Groomsmen (and/or ushers) arrive about two hours before the ceremony in order to seat guests.

2. The music begins about thirty minutes before the ceremony.

3. The candles, if any, are lit after the music begins. (Your clergy person or wedding consultant will guide you here.)

4. Guests may indicate that they wish to sit on the bride's side (the left) or the groom's (the right). (In an Orthodox or Conservative Jewish ceremony, the bride's and groom's sides are reversed.) If either the bride's or the groom's side has more family and guests than the other, then this tradition need not be followed and ushers seat guests randomly to fill the church or wedding site.

5. Relatives and honored guests are seated at the front in the bride's section (on the left) or the groom's (on the right). Stepmothers are considered honored guests who are seated in the second or third rows. If the families do not get along, the stepmothers are seated farther back in the church on the proper side.

6. Seating of the families starts about ten minutes before the ceremony begins. The grandparents of the groom and then the grandparents of the bride are seated.

7. The mother of the groom is seated and then the mother of the bride. No one is escorted to a seat after the mothers are seated. Latecomers must sit in the back of the church or in the balcony.

8. At the hour of the wedding, the processional begins. This parade is actually a liturgical procession. If there is to be special music, it takes place just before the processional. (The selection and timing should be at the guidance of wedding-site personnel.)

9. The officiant enters, usually from the right, leading the way for the groom and the best man.

10. The groomsmen enter one by one or two by two and take their places.

11. The bridesmaids enter one by one or two by two and take their places.

12. The honor attendants—maid of honor first, then the matron— enter and take their places on the left.

13. The ring bearer comes down the aisle and stands with the men.

14. The flower girl enters and stands beside the honor attendants.

15. If this is a custom in your community, the mother of the bride rises and all of the guests stand.

16. The music the bride has chosen for her processional begins. The guests get teary as the bride enters on her father's left arm. (If she wishes, the bride may walk down the aisle alone, with her father and/or mother, with her brother, or with another male relative.)

Alone at Last

Jewish newlyweds usually spend about ten or fifteen minutes alone after the ceremony. This time-out, called the *Yichod*, originally was when the couple consummated their marriage. Today, couples so appreciate the breather before plunging into reception festivities that many non-Jewish brides and grooms are adopting it.

17. The father remains with the bride until he is asked, "Who giveth this woman to be married to this man?" After answering, he may kiss his daughter and then sits with the bride's mother in the first row or in the third row with his wife, the bride's stepmother. (If the couple opts to omit this tradition, the bride is escorted to the groom's side and whoever is accompanying her sits down.)

18. The ceremony begins. The groom assists the bride going up or down any steps at the altar. The maid or matron of honor arranges the bride's train.

19. The maid or matron of honor holds the bride's bouquet during the service as needed. She also may lift the bride's blush veil, if she has one, at the appropriate time, although many couples prefer for the groom to do this.

20. The ceremony ends with the bride and groom having their first kiss as newlyweds.

21. The music swells into the recessional, and the couple turns and goes back up the aisle.

22. The child attendants follow the bride and groom.

23. The maid or matron of honor takes the right arm of the best man, and they exit. If there are two honor attendants, the best man may escort them both or the maid of honor may exit with a groomsman.

24. The rest of the bridesmaids and groomsmen pair up and exit. (If the couple prefers or if the number of men and women in the wedding party is uneven, the bridesmaids may leave in pairs, followed by pairs of groomsmen.)

25. Guests remain seated until the mothers and grandmothers are escorted out by groomsmen. This is done in the reverse order than they were seated. If the mothers (and grandmothers) have remarried, their husbands follow the women and their escorts.

26. Stepmothers are considered guests and leave with their husbands when the guests leave—unless the bride and groom wish for them to be escorted by groomsmen. Their husbands would follow them.

27. The officiant usually exits when the guests rise to leave. He may signal them to rise.

A Word About the Catholic Service

The Catholic service may or may not include a Mass. The Mass (Eucharist) is given after the exchange of vows and rings. The service ends with the nuptial blessing.

According to Catholic liturgy and theology, a woman is never given in marriage. Marriage is a holy state, freely entered by the man and the woman. So, although a woman is usually escorted down the aisle by her father, the priest never asks who gives her in marriage. In some cases, the bridegroom takes a step or two toward the bride to signify that he also enters the union freely and willingly.

For more information, please see the chapter titled Divorce and Religion.

CEREMONY COUNTDOWN FOR SECOND MARRIAGES (CHRISTIAN)

A bride having a large wedding with all the trimmings, even though she may be marrying for the second time, follows the ceremony format above. The second-time bride who prefers a less lavish wedding may follow the format below. Please note that although there is no formal processional, the couple still may walk down the aisle if they choose.

1. Guests begin arriving and seat themselves, unless there are ushers available. The first rows are marked with bows indicating they are reserved for family. Stepmothers are considered guests and are not seated formally.

2. The mothers are escorted by their husbands and seated. If the groom wishes to escort his mother, he may do so.

3. At the hour of the wedding, the bride and groom, with their attendants, emerge from either side of the room and gather in front of the officiant.

4. If the couple's children are taking part in the ceremony, the couple may have a small processional. The boys come down the aisle first, then the girls. The bride's children stand on the left, the groom's on the right.

5. The flower girl comes down the aisle and stands on the left.

6. If she wishes, the bride may walk down the aisle alone, with her father and/or mother, her brother, with a teenaged or older son, or with the groom.

7. The bride's escort, if he is not the groom, gives her hand to the groom and sits down. The traditional question, "Who giveth this woman to be married to this man?" is inappropriate when the bride has been married before, but it may be asked if the officiant allows it.

8. The ceremony ends with the bride and groom having their first kiss as newlyweds.

9. The couple turns to hug and kiss their children.

10. They may greet well-wishers where they stand or they may make a more formal exit up the aisle.

11. The children join arms and follow their parents out of the church.

All of the above is quite informal and should be adjusted to suit each family's situation. If the flower girl or the ring bearer is very young, the bride and groom may hold the child's hands and the three exit together. Whatever works for them as a family is best.

The Jewish Ceremony: Under the Chuppah

In the Jewish faith, marriage is seen as a sanctification of life and a consecration of self toward noble ends. According to Helen Latner, author of *Your Jewish Wedding*, the married state is a "basic social institution that contributes to society through the founding of a home and a family."

Each of the three major religious points of view—Orthodox, Conservative, and Reform—interprets the requirements and procedures for marriage slightly differently. A couple should consult their rabbi before setting a date because marriages are forbidden on certain days of the year, such as the Sabbath, holy days and festivals, or other special times.

Whether held in a synagogue, a hotel, club, or home, the Jewish wedding ceremony is filled with symbolism and tradition. One of the most distinctive parts of the ceremony is the marriage canopy, or *chuppah* (or *huppah*), which is often lavishly decorated with flowers. The couple stands under the chuppah, which symbolizes the home (or, according to some, the bridal chamber) and the unity of the marriage.

Before the ceremony begins, the couple signs a *ketubbah* (or *ketubah*). The Jewish equivalent of the marriage contract, this document outlines the obligations and responsibilities of the bride and groom and is given to the bride for safekeeping.

Another ceremony that the couple may perform before the ceremony has its roots in the story of Jacob, who loved Rachel. After working for seven years to marry her, he was tricked by Rachel's father, who substituted her heavily veiled sister, Leah, at the wedding. The story survives in the Jewish tradition of "covering the bride," where the groom lowers her blush veil himself before the ceremony begins.

The breaking of a wineglass at the conclusion of the service is another distinctive tradition practiced at most Jewish ceremonies. With his right foot, the groom smashes a wineglass wrapped in a linen napkin. It is often said that the breaking of the glass signifies the destruction of the first temple in Jerusalem. Another explanation of the rite is that it reminds us in a time of happiness that life is fragile.

Another lovely tradition, one that has been borrowed by many non-Jewish brides, is the custom of having the bride's and groom's parents accompany them in the processional. In Jewish weddings, grandparents are included as well, because the Jewish wedding is seen as the joining of two families.

Although there is no set order, most processionals traditionally are as follows:

1. The rabbi and/or cantor
2. Grandparents of the groom
3. Groomsmen (if any)
4. Best man
5. The groom, escorted by his father on his left and his mother on his right
6. Grandparents of the bride
7. Bridesmaids (if any)
8. Maid or matron of honor
9. Flower girl
10. The bride, escorted by her father on her left and her mother on her right

> If the grandparents are quite elderly, they may be assisted by a grandchild. ०४०

In Orthodox ceremonies, the two fathers may escort the groom and the two mothers, the bride. The best man leads the ushers, and the maid of honor leads the bridesmaids.

The rabbi, bride, and groom stand under the chuppah, the groom's family to the left and the bride's family to the right. Wedding planner

Sue Winner, of Sue Winner Associates in Atlanta, likes to describe the chuppah as representing the couple's home, with the parents flanking it like supporting walls. The grandparents may stand or sit under the canopy or in the first row of seats.

The wedding party exits in this order:

1. Bride and groom
2. The bride's parents
3. The groom's parents
4. The maid of honor and the best man
5. Flower girl
6. The rabbi and/or cantor

When the Parents Are Divorced

In the case of divorce, parents should put aside any differences and escort their child to the chuppah. If either has remarried, the new spouse does not participate but sits with the other guests.

When the atmosphere is hostile and the ex-spouse is not invited to the wedding, the mother or father may escort his or her child without a partner. If the parent has remarried and the bride or groom is close to the new spouse, it is permissible to ask the stepparent to participate in the wedding.

In families where the parents have divorced and remarried, the parents of the bride or groom's stepparents do not walk in the processional. Only the grandparents in the original family are so honored. In complicated situations where there are several sets of grandparents, it is permissible to omit them all from the processional. They would be seated in the family rows.

When the Bride or Groom Is Divorced

In order to remarry in a Jewish ceremony, a divorced person must receive a *Get*, or religious divorce.

Children

Kid-Friendly Weddings

While a second-time wedding frequently creates an instant family—just add champagne—it may not be a happy union, especially in the beginning. Children can be a major cause of the dissolution of second marriages.

Often after a divorce, one spouse is still bitter and angry. Sometimes the children are, too. Perhaps a child resents a parent's new girlfriend or boyfriend—or worse, the new love is the one who broke up the original family. The universal dream of children of divorced parents is that Mom and Dad will get back together. It can be crushing to a child when that hope is finally shattered.

A new engagement ring is a symbol of a new unity between two people, and children may feel excluded. We know one woman in her thirties who is still hurt that she was not part of her mother's second marriage twenty-two years ago. "That psychologically is very unfortunate because you never feel like part of the union," she said. This woman was a victim of the antiquated rule of etiquette that children from a first marriage should be neither seen nor heard at subsequent ones, as if they were a dirty secret that should be hidden.

Today, people know that children should be included in weddings—and wedding preparations—if they choose. If the new husband or wife was involved in the dissolution of the original marriage, then it is cruel to expect children to participate.

When the two of you realize your romance could lead to a lifetime commitment, you can prepare your children gradually for the possibility of remarriage by taking the following steps.

• Once it is clear that the relationship is serious, the new lover and the children should be given a chance to get to know each other, and he or she should be included in family activities.

• Parents should openly display affection toward their intended. We're not talking about the sloppy PDAs (public displays of affection) that our mothers frowned on. But hand-holding and hugs are important to let a child know that this relationship is serious. This is also a way to stress to a child that divorce does not kill loving feelings no matter how badly it hurt, and that there is always hope for love.

• Parents should bring up the subject of remarriage occasionally in conversation. This is a chance to find out how the kids feel.

• When a couple decides to marry, their children should be the first to know of the engagement.

• Parents should involve the children in any wedding preparations, offering them limited choices on anything from clothing to menus, for example, "Do you think the wedding cake should be carrot or chocolate?"

Some of the suggestions may not be workable, but couples should consider their children's ideas. Compromise where necessary. One might not think the *Lion King* theme appropriate for a wedding, but music from the show could be played for dancing during the reception.

If they choose, the children should be part of the wedding party. Flower girls, ring bearers, and bridesmaids are obvious choices, but couples serious about including their children can find innovative options. Some second-time brides have been escorted by their teenaged sons, and fathers have asked sons to stand in as best man.

Making children part of the actual wedding ceremony is becoming popular. While couples might not want to go as far as making their children exchange rings or be pronounced "husband, wife, and children"—as some blended families have—they may want to consider letting the children stand with them or do special readings.

LOVE HANDLES

Some etiquette manuals advise couples to leave the groom's kids out of the ceremony if they don't fit into the first-time bride's plans for a dream wedding. Maybe his daughters are too old to be classified as junior bridesmaids. Maybe the bride already asked her friends to be attendants and she doesn't need more. Maybe she already has a ring bearer.

> ∞ "We are all God's children—by a previous marriage."
> —*Graffiti*

Whatever the problem, the reasoning is that the bride deserves to get what she wants because she's the bride, so there. Wrong! Instead, she may get what she *deserves*: hurt children who feel she doesn't care about them.

A wedding is a wonderful opportunity to forge new ties with the people who will be family after the "I do's" are over. The gracious bride knows it's a shame to waste it.

A bride writes: I am an older bride who doesn't know whom to include in her wedding party. My fiancé's twelve-year-old daughter wants to be the flower

girl. Isn't she too old? I have a seven-year-old adopted son I would like to have give me away. I have two older sons, but to choose one would hurt the other. Is this OK? And I have a future sister-in-law whom I want to include in the wedding. I also wanted to ask one daughter-in-law, but what about my other daughter-in-law? I don't want hurt feelings. We will be married at home.
—RELATIVELY SPEAKING

DEAR RELATIVELY: Since this will be an at-home family affair, have them all. To leave anyone out would only cause hurt feelings.

You may have your youngest son escort you down the aisle or you may walk alone, letting your children proceed you. However, it is inappropriate for young children to "give" their mother away.

A bride writes: My fiancé has an eleven-year-old daughter from his first marriage. His daughter and I are close, and I plan to ask her to be a junior bridesmaid, but I am not familiar with all the details. Where does she walk in the processional and the recessional? Would she walk with a groomsman? Do I invite her to a shower? —REACHING OUT

DEAR REACHING: Including your fiancé's daughter in the wedding is a terrific idea. Children from other marriages were once all but ignored when their parents remarried. Including them is a good first step to creating a new family.

The bride and groom who want to include young children in their wedding may consider having tiny chairs at the front for the youngsters. ∞

A junior bridesmaid wears a dress similar to that of the bridesmaids, yet suitable for her age. Her primary duty is to walk in the processional and look adorable. She precedes the bridesmaids down the aisle. During the recessional, she may walk alone or with a groomsman—usually a big thrill for a young girl. She need not attend showers (unless she wishes) nor contribute to the gift from the bridesmaids.

A bride writes: My fiancé and I would like to invite his two nieces, ages eleven and nine, to be in the wedding. The problem is that they live in another state with their mother. When my fiancé's family want to see the children, they have to make the three-hour drive each way to pick up the children and bring them back. Their mother does not allow the girls to fly. My fiancé and his family don't want the children's mother to attend the wedding. Should the children be invited without their mother? —Bewildered Bride

Dear Bewildered: Given the animosity in this family, you need not invite the girls' mother, but your fiancé's brother or mother will have to be in charge of them for the weekend. If the mother will still not allow the girls to fly, then someone will have to make the trek to pick them up. It stands to reason that your fiancé's brother should make the transportation arrangements, if he can.

Relatively Speaking

Introductions to people in families that have undergone divorce can get crazy. It's difficult to know what to call relatives when one isn't sure just who the relatives *are*.

And if it's hard for adults, just imagine how overwhelmed children can feel. It's best not to pressure them into using intimate names if they don't feel comfortable. For example, if a child already has two grandmothers, choose a special nickname for granddad's new wife or for his new stepfather's mother.

When it comes to blended families, thoughtful parents will introduce the children—his, hers, and theirs—as "our children," making no distinctions between them, if the kids are comfortable with this.

Clothing

Dressing the Part

*L*et's face it. Part of the fun of getting married is getting to wear fabulous clothes that make us feel elegant and special. For most of us, formal wear is not part of our daily lives, so dressing up also signifies the importance and solemnity of the wedding ritual.

The proper attire for a wedding depends upon its formality and the time it will take place. This section will help guide you through the mysteries of proper wedding attire.

THE BRIDE'S ATTIRE

"White, my dears, is reserved for first-time brides." For decades, this was the rule, so sayeth the wedding-etiquette experts. Although these women didn't dare mention the "V" word, it was implicit that white was only for virginal brides. If you weren't a virgin, you couldn't wear white, and many a bride felt guilty on her wedding day for the hypocrisy of white, rather than let everyone in town know she'd given in to natural urges many months before the wedding.

And when you married again, whether after divorce or death, your color was pastel blue or pink, if you please.

Today, all of that is so yesterday. So many second-time brides let their burning desire to wear the dress of a lifetime—that satin wedding cake of a gown—overcome any fears of ridicule and now white is no longer taboo. One bride told me that she could wear white again because this was the first time she was marrying the man she loved. Women have also been told by so-called etiquette experts that if their hearts are "pure" this time around, those previous marriages don't count and it is OK to wear white.

I don't buy that line. Tradition ought to mean something. But, to me the issue is not so much color as *style*.

Brides come in only two models: young, i.e, "inexperienced," and mature, or experienced, although I prefer the description "older and, hopefully, wiser." The young and inexperienced bride gets to wear a white, froufrou gown complete with train and veil, while the mature bride prefers a sleeker, more sophisticated look. Besides, at her age, ivory is more flattering.

Is practicality an issue? Then a suit or tea-length gown is the most appropriate attire for second-time brides. Who wants to spend a fortune on an elaborate dress that's worn just one time? Certainly our grandmothers didn't. That kind of wedding dress is an expensive

 ## Still Off Limits: A Veil

Sorry, but a veil still signifies virginity. A hat or no headpiece at all is best, unless you can't resist the urge to "wear some flowers in your hair."

post–World War II trend in wealthy industrialized nations. The more mature bride—who often faces paying for orthodontics or college while she's planning another wedding—also knows she'll get more wear out of an elegant suit or evening gown than a frilly wedding dress.

The best reason for forgoing the flounces and ruffles? They look silly on all but the very young. The second-time bride should go for sexy and sophisticated instead.

A bride writes: Is it considered gauche to wear the same gown again? This gown was one my mother and I loved. I never tried on another one. Now she has passed away. It's funny, but I relate this dress to her, not my former husband. —SECOND-TIME BRIDE

DEAR SECOND-TIMER: Most people would consider wearing the same wedding dress unlucky. Others who remember your dress might call wearing it again tacky. But my thought is that since your wedding is a smaller affair, you would want a dress or suit that is more appropriate than a wedding gown with all the bells and whistles. Besides, what would your fiancé think? Would *he* like to see you drift down the aisle in a gown that you once wore for another man? Would you like him to wear the special cuff links that were an anniversary gift from his former wife?

A bride writes: This is my second marriage after having been divorced for two years. I want to wear a white dress. Is this appropriate? My fiancé wants to wear a white tuxedo. Is this appropriate for a late morning–early afternoon wedding? —WHITE ON WHITE

DEAR WHITE: It's more acceptable for you to wear a white gown than for your fiancé to show up in a white tuxedo. Proper attire for a morning wedding is a black or gray cutaway or stroller. Tuxedos are after-eight attire, and white tuxedos are never-never attire. Remember, you don't want to be embarrassed by your wedding photos in twenty years with attire that was a bad fad.

If you do opt for a white dress, pick one with pastel touches and forgo the long veil and train. Those are for first-time brides.

A bride writes: I am to be married in an informal to semiformal wedding in late May. This will be my second wedding, and I don't know what type of dress is appropriate. My fiancé is no help. His taste runs to tight, black leather miniskirts. He does like backless or off-the-shoulder styles. He loves to see me in white, but I am not sure if I should wear white. I am totally at a loss to choose the one perfect dress for this occasion. —DRESS BLUES

DEAR DRESS: A bride's attire is supposed to project an image of chaste purity. Anything lustier must wait until you two are alone. So leave your fiancé at home when you go shopping or you're liable to end up in white leather.

An elegant suit in white or off-white is always appropriate for an informal or semiformal wedding. By happy chance, that is also the correct attire for a second-time bride.

Lifesavers

- Whether you are wearing your mother's gown or buying a dress off the rack of your favorite boutique, you still may need to schedule fittings with a reputable seamstress.
- If you are pregnant, tell the fitter at your first appointment.
- Pack an emergency kit—hose, cosmetics, safety pins, needle and thread, nail file, tissue, extra slip—to take to the ceremony and reception. Also include Shout damp wipes. They're excellent for removing lipstick and other stains.

MOTHERS AND STEPMOTHERS

Here's where the gloves come off. Blame it on human nature, but when it comes to selecting their wedding outfits, a little bit of competitiveness often develops between the bride's or groom's mother and her ex-husband's subsequent wife. All right, *a lot* of competitiveness.

Like the mother of the groom, the stepmother should take her wardrobe cues from the mother of the bride. And while a stepmom wants to look her best, she should not try to outdo the mothers of the couple on their wedding day. A wedding is not the appropriate time for a subsequent wife to outshine the mother of the bride or groom. Instead, she should take a gracious and retiring role or risk losing the respect of her stepchildren and others in her husband's family. Only a petty, selfish person would stoop so low.

Then there was the mother of the bride who learned that her ex-husband's new trophy wife had selected the same designer dress as she was planning to wear to the wedding. "What did you do?" she was asked. "I wore the dress to the rehearsal dinner the night before," the quick-witted lady cooed.

A bride writes: My stepmother and I don't know what color is appropriate for her to wear. Should she be different from my mother? My attendants are wearing soft pink. My mother also might wear this color. Does it matter whether they are the same or different? —COLOR CODED

 ## Is She or Isn't She?

The mothers and stepmothers of the bride and groom are not considered part of the wedding party, so their outfits need not color-coordinate with the bridesmaids' dresses. But their dresses should be complementing styles, for example, casual or formal, long or short. However, if Mom has the legs for a miniskirt, she should go for it.

Dear Color Coded: Your stepmother should not try to upstage your mother. She should avoid wearing the color that your mom has selected. Her outfit should not draw comment.

ATTENDANTS

There is one line every woman who's ever been a bridesmaid has heard: "And you'll be able to wear this dress again!" Yeah, right. Well-meaning brides continually try to come up with a style for their attendants to wear that is tasteful and fashionable, looks good on six different body shapes, yet is affordable. Oh, and it can't look like the typical "bridesmaids dress" either.

While some brides come close, most fail miserably. These are mutually exclusive requirements. I attended one wedding where the bridesmaids were garbed in hideous dresses with big flowers all over them. The wedding party looked like a sectional sofa.

Here are the rules for selecting your attendants' attire:

• The style of the dress or outfit should match the style of the wedding. For example, a formal evening wedding calls for a long, formal gown.

• Choose classic, not trendy, if, years from now, you don't want your children to laugh at pictures of Mom and Dad on their wedding day.

• Select fabrics that suit the season. Velvet is not the fabric for an outdoor wedding in the spring but works well for a late fall or winter wedding. Linen says summer.

• Black, as we all know by now, is fine, but colorful clothing is more fun and your wedding will look more festive. However, stay away from trendy colors such as Day-Glo orange or neon green that will date your wedding.

• Some churches have restrictions on bare shoulders and revealing décolleté. Look for gowns that come with jackets or stoles that can be removed at the reception.

Which One Is the Maid of Honor?

A trend that seems to come and go periodically has the maid or matron of honor dressed differently from the other women in the wedding party. It's not necessary, but a bride certainly may do this if she chooses.

Junior Bridesmaids

Junior bridesmaids are usually the bride's or groom's sisters or nieces between the ages of twelve and fourteen. In the case of women or men who have been married previously, their teenaged daughters may act as a junior bridesmaid.

Junior bridesmaids wear dresses similar to those worn by the bridesmaids, although if the dresses are strapless or décolleté, they may be altered so that they are more age-appropriate.

How to Make Your Attendants Happy

Second-time brides usually have only one or two attendants. Instead of requiring them to dress like twins, the more sophisticated bride allows her attendants to decide what they will wear, as long as it is in keeping with the style of the wedding. (One wouldn't want an attendant in a miniskirt while the bride wears a long gown.) Another approach is to select the fabric, supply a seamstress, and allow each attendant to select a style flattering to her.

Whichever approach, the smart bride *always* maintains veto power.

Flower Girls and Ring Bearers

Clothing for the younger set should be—in a word—sweet. Lace- or ribbon-trimmed party frocks for the little girls, who also may wear halos of flowers or big bows in their hair. Colors should be white or pastels, accented with colors from the wedding party. Shoes should be Sunday school best in black patent or white leather.

They hate them, but little boys look so angelic in shorts and knee-socks paired with a short Eton jacket. They wear white in summer and dark in winter with matching shoes.

In addition to a flower girl and ring bearer, some couples add a miniature bride and bridegroom, who dress like tiny versions of the adults. Considered cute in some circles and tacky in others, the smart bride will veto this idea—too easy to be upstaged!

The Groom and Groomsmen

Clothing for the men in the wedding party is terribly complicated, ranging from white tie for formal, evening weddings to cutaways and strollers at formal, daytime weddings to dinner jackets and tuxedos at semiformal, evening weddings. Informal, daytime weddings call for dark suits in the winter and navy blazers with light trousers in the summer.

*A bride writes: I am confused about the wedding attire. Do all the brides-maids have to wear the same style of dress or can they differ? Is it true that the flower girl wears a dress that duplicates my gown? What kind of dress can the maid of honor wear: similar to the bridesmaids' or something different? Do the mothers wear custom-made dresses? Are their styles similar or totally different? —*Dressing Up

Dear Dressing: The bridesmaids usually wear similar dresses, although this is not required. In smaller weddings or in second weddings, brides often tell their attendants to select something in the same color range. The maid of honor should wear a dress similar to the bridesmaids.

The flower girl should not look like a miniature bride but should be dressed in something charming and innocent that picks up the colors of the bridesmaids' dresses.

The mothers are not considered part of the wedding party and should not try to dress like the bridesmaids. Their gowns need not be custom designed. The only "rule" for the mothers is that their dresses are similar in degree of formality. For instance, you wouldn't want one

 ## Wedding Style

The formality of a wedding is determined by the bride's dress and the time of day (before or after six o'clock). These guidelines apply to first marriages but may be adapted for subsequent marriages:

Informal: Daytime or Evening
- Bride: Tea-length gown or dressy suit. Short veil, hat, or flowers.
- Groom: Dark suit in fall or winter. White suit in summer or navy blue blazer with white, gray, or tan trousers. Conservative four-in-hand tie.

Semiformal: Daytime
- Bride: Tea-length gown or gown with short train. Elbow-length veil.
- Groom: Oxford gray or black stroller coat. Gray or black striped pants. Gray vest. Gray silk four-in-hand tie.

Semiformal: Evening
- Bride: Floor-length gown or gown with short train. Elbow or fingertip veil.
- Groom: Black tuxedo or white dinner jacket with tuxedo pants. Black tie and cummerbund.

mother in sequins while the other looks as though she dressed for the office. And yes, they both may wear the same color. If they both like blue, let them wear blue. By the way, the bride's mother, who is hostess, selects her gown first. The mother of the groom takes her fashion cues from the bride's mother.

A bride writes: Is it permissible for my fiancé to be dressed differently from the other men in the wedding so he will stand out? —FASHION CONSCIOUS

DEAR FASHION CONSCIOUS: Only if you don't think you will recognize him.

Formal: Daytime
- Bride: Floor-length gown with cathedral or sweep train. Fingertip or longer veil.
- Groom: Gray or black cutaway or stroller. Striped trousers. Gray or white vest. Gray ascot or four-in-hand tie.

Formal: Evening
- Bride: Floor-length gown with short, sweep, or cathedral train. Fingertip or longer veil.
- Groom: Black tails and matching pants. White tie and vest.

Ultraformal: Daytime
- Bride: Full-length gown with cathedral or shorter train. Long or fingertip veil.
- Groom: Cutaway or stroller coat with striped trousers and striped or white linen vest. Gray ascot or four-in-hand tie.

Ultraformal: Evening
- Bride: Full-length gown with cathedral or shorter train. Long or fingertip veil.
- Groom: Black tails and matching pants. White tie. White pique vest.

Computers and
Your Wedding

Technically Speaking

*S*avvy couples turn to their home computers to help keep their wedding planning organized. Many couples have found that setting up their own Web page is a great way to keep attendants and guests apprised of wedding-weekend activities or hotel accommodations. Internet registries make it easy for guests who live out of state to find a gift that's sure to be "just what the bride and groom wanted."

Couples use their home computers to design their wedding programs and keep up with their guest lists and gift records. (Please see the chapter called Guest List and Gift Record.) The Internet is also a great resource to find wedding vendors and research bridal trends. And what bride can get along without E-mail to keep her mom and her attendants "in the loop" on wedding planning?

Bad Bytes

When you are getting married, some old-fashioned ways are still the best.

• Never use computer-printed address labels for your wedding invitations. This is the most important social occasion of your life. Don't cheapen it with tacky labels.

• Don't believe everything you read on the Internet. There are plenty of websites where wedding "experts" dispense advice willy-nilly. But most of them are trying to sell you something. Think twice before following their advice when your best instincts tell you it's not a gracious way to act.

• Be careful when ordering from on-line vendors. Your wedding won't be a disaster if your personalized soap bubbles don't arrive in time for your big day, but a missing wedding dress is another matter.

• Do not E-mail thank-you notes. They must be handwritten and hand-addressed by the bride and groom.

Consultants

"Help! I Need Somebody"

$\mathcal{W}$ith the average price of weddings reaching $20,000, mistakes and fraud can potentially add thousands more to an already expensive affair. But most couples will agree that the worst cost is the embarrassment when what should have been a wonderful occasion goes horribly awry. What are the bride and groom to do?

Wedding consultants can provide couples with a priceless service—peace of mind on a nerve-wracking day. They work with reputable vendors with whom they do business on a regular basis, and they know the ins and outs of contracts. For example, some caterers charge extra for forks, a cost that catches some brides and grooms by surprise.

A consultant's research can save busy couples time and money. For example, a wedding consultant will match the wedding size and budget to an appropriate site. One Atlanta bride said her consultant saved her money by steering her to an elegant restaurant that she would never have considered. "With the restaurant's gorgeous décor, my wedding was a lot more tasteful and special than if we had held it in a hotel ballroom," she said. "Plus the food was fantastic."

For the couple who wants to do everything themselves, some consultants are available to help coordinate the wedding day itself. It may be worth turning those last-minute details over to someone else who will make sure that the photographer gets the right people in the photos and that the caterer begins serving on time.

Consultants either charge by the hour or as a percentage of your wedding. The best way to find a consultant is word of mouth. Ask friends. Some churches and synagogues have lists of approved consultants. Some consultants also register with the Association of Bridal Consultants (203-355-0464), but that is a professional organization that does not license or train consultants.

Is a Wedding Consultant for You?

Are you planning a wedding that will be held in a different city or state? Do you have an extremely time-consuming career or family? Does your guest list include hundreds of people? Will your wedding take place at a site that makes planning it complicated? Then a wedding consultant may be what you need.

If you are considering hiring a consultant, remember:

- Like interior designers, they are to guide you, not dictate your wedding style. If you feel that your thoughts and wishes are being ignored, find another consultant.
- No matter how good they are and how much experience they have had, they are not etiquette experts. When in doubt, ask yourself what is the most gracious thing to do, then do it.

Deceased Parents

On a Sad Note

*T*he wedding day can be especially poignant for the bride or groom who has lost a beloved parent or stepparent. Couples who have lost a loved one just weeks before the wedding may wish to delay the ceremony. Many couples wish to make some remembrance of the deceased, but these are inappropriate as an overt part of the wedding. Here are some suggestions for honoring deceased parents gracefully.

A toast at the rehearsal dinner. A rehearsal dinner is an intimate, emotional setting, and a mention of the deceased in a loving way during a toast of the couple would be appreciated by all. Toast the couple, saying how proud the deceased would be to see his daughter (her son) marrying so happily.

A memento of the deceased. One groom told me that carrying his late father's pocket watch made him feel his father's presence with him throughout the ceremony. One bride wore her late mother's pearl necklace.

A prayer. During the ceremony, have the officiant lead a prayer that mentions the deceased.

A candle. Burn a candle in the deceased's memory.

A dedication. Mention in the program that the floral decorations are in memory of the deceased.

A bride writes: My fiancé's mother died when he was eleven years old (he is now twenty-seven). His father remarried only two years ago. The groom-to-be wants his stepmother to be treated like a mother at the wedding, but he also doesn't want his own mother to be forgotten. How do we word the invitations if both sets of parents will be included on the invitations? —NOT FORGOTTEN

DEAR FORGOTTEN: This may sound harsh, but a wedding is not a memorial service. It is a happy time, and mentioning your fiancé's deceased mother on the invitation—however noble his motives—should not be done.

However, her name should be included in the announcement for the newspapers.

It is perfectly acceptable for you to include his father and step-mother on the invitation. The wording would be:

Mr. and Mrs. William Boyle McCoy
request the honour of your presence
at the marriage of their daughter
Eilene Shannon

to

Mr. Neill Kemper Leake Jr.
son of
Mr. and Mrs. Neill Kemper Leake [the groom's father and his new wife]
[and so forth]

If your fiancé still wishes to honor his mother, do it with dignity. A donation in her name to the church, a single rosebud on the altar during the ceremony, or a prayer in her memory could be his special remembrance of her. The remembrance could be explained in the program.

*A bride writes: My fiancé and I have been together for six years. We have two children and own our home. I guess you could say that the wedding is just a formality. You could also say that we don't pattern our lives by tradition or any type of rules. We will have a small ceremony, and I plan to wear a nice dress instead of a traditional wedding gown. Both of our mothers are deceased. We would like to honor our mothers by having white roses placed on the front rows in their memory. We would put a note in the program explaining this to the guests. Is this an OK idea? How should we include my fiancé's step-mother? —*AT LAST

DEAR AT LAST: Tributes to deceased parents have become trendy, but I think some are in poor taste. I empathize with a couple's wish to remember their beloved parents on one of the most important days of their lives, but a public display—whether it is interrupting the ceremony to light candles or to lay flowers where the mother would have been seated—seems insincere and overly sentimental to me. Besides, a wedding day is supposed to be a time of great joy, untouched by thoughts of death. If you feel there is a need to recognize deceased parents, perhaps you are having the wedding too soon after the funeral.

Instead, I prefer to see couples make a private tribute, by carrying or wearing something that belonged to the deceased or perhaps in a private prayer with the officiant. The minister may also remember the departed in a prayer during the ceremony.

Your proposal also complicates seating for your families. As the wife of your fiancé's father, his stepmother's place is on the front row. Forcing her to share a row with a floral tribute to her predecessor is inconsiderate.

Disasters and How to Prevent Them

*N*o matter how well you plan, disasters can happen. But if you are prepared for the unexpected, you two will someday remember these "disasters" as fond memories that delight your children. Believe it or not, all of the following actually happened to brides and grooms. After all, there is no such thing as a perfect wedding.

THE CLOTHING

"I took friends to see my dress, and the shop was out of business!" Avoid this nightmare by depending on a reputable bridal salon that has been in business for years. Discount dealers may save you money initially but can be painfully expensive in the long run, especially if the dress

of the bride's dreams is not available. *Always* shop with a credit card because if the shop goes out of business or the order is unsatisfactory, you can contest the charge within ninety days. If you write a check and the shop closes, you have lost your money.

"My gown didn't arrive until the day of my wedding!" Again, go with a reputable salon. And the bride should give herself plenty of time. Six months is considered a minimum lead time. Arrange for delivery several months before the wedding.

"I was getting dressed at the church, and I stepped on the hem of my gown and ripped it!" Brides, take an emergency kit with hose, needle and thread, pins, scissors, deodorant, tampons, mouthwash, and anything you could possibly need to the wedding site.

"I forgot my shoes and had to wear my sneakers!" The week before the wedding, make a list of everything that must go with you to the wedding site. Refer to the list as you pack.

"The tuxedo rental company short-changed us one pair of black patent shoes!" Always check your order immediately, whether it's the bride's gown, the men's clothing, or the flowers. Be ready to improvise, if needed.

THE CEREMONY

"The bridesmaids were late getting to the church so the wedding started late!" Give everyone a schedule showing where he or she should be at a specific time, for example:

Bridesmaids

    2:30 P.M.—Leave the hotel

    3:00 P.M.—Arrive at the church

    3:00–4:00 P.M.—Dress and do makeup

    4:00–4:55 P.M.—Photos in the church courtyard

    4:55 P.M.—Gather outside sanctuary

    5:00 P.M.—Wedding begins

Groomsmen

    3:00 P.M.—Arrive at church courtyard for photos

    4:00 P.M.—Gather at front door to seat early arrivals

    5:00 P.M.—Wedding begins

"The groom fainted!" You can't head off a bad case of nerves, but you can make sure everyone has eaten something before the wedding. And your wedding party will look and feel more chipper if you keep the rehearsal dinner from degenerating into a rowdy late-night party.

"The flower girl refused to walk down the aisle, and guests could hear her howling and crying!" Children are always going to be an unknown entity. Etiquette expert that I am, I am still known in certain family circles as a reprobate flower girl who announced to the entire church "I have to tee-tee" at a cousin's wedding more than forty years ago. There is only way to ensure that a flower girl or ring bearer won't "mess up" your wedding: don't have kids in it. If you do decide to have a flower girl or ring bearer, make sure your sense of humor is in good working order.

"The ring bearer drop kicked his pillow and then began running up and down the aisle!" Always have a backup plan. Have an adult ready to grab any wayward little ones and spirit them out of the church. Think long and hard about having a child participate if you are the kind of person bothered by kids acting like kids. And this should be a reminder

to make sure the real rings are safely in the keeping of the maid of honor and the best man. Fake rings should be sewn onto the pillow—just in case it becomes a football.

"We forgot Grandma and left her at the church so she had to take a cab to the reception!" Make sure any honored guests, particularly if they are elderly, have escorts to the church and the reception.

The Food

"The food tasted terrible!" Ask to sample the dishes before you sign the contract with the caterer or reception hall.

"This wasn't what we ordered!" If the caterer reserves the right to make last-minute substitutions in the menu depending on what's available, insist on a clause saying he must notify you of any changes. (Follow the same procedure with the florist.)

The Flowers

"My bouquet was so heavy that it fell apart!" Ask to see a sample of the bouquet. Make sure it will hold up throughout the ceremony and reception.

"We were short three boutonnieres!" Appoint a friend to be in charge of flowers, whether they are delivered or picked up. Make sure your order is complete before signing off on the delivery. If this problem is not caught until too late for replacements to be made, send all of the men—except for the groom and the best man—down the aisle without them.

THE MUSIC

"The band was horrible . . . too loud and they couldn't keep a beat!" Instead of relying upon tapes or videos of a band, go hear the group at another wedding. Look for a group that plays together regularly, not a band of pickup musicians who will not sound polished. Your contract should stipulate the names of the musicians. One couple hired a band with a great singer, but when the band arrived at their reception, the desired singer had been replaced.

"The deejay played heavy metal songs that I hated!" Make sure that the deejay or the band plays the *style* of music you like. Also make sure that the deejay or band has a playlist of the specific songs with the artists you want and when to play them. This does not always guarantee that the deejay or band will honor your wishes. You may want to have this stipulated in the contract. Also, give a friend or your wedding coordinator an extra copy of your instructions—just in case.

"During our first dance together, the deejay played some horrible song about sex. I was so embarrassed!" Again, communicate your wishes to the band or deejay ahead of time in writing.

"The band played throughout dinner and then quit for a thirty-minute break just as people were ready to dance. It brought the reception to a standstill!" Stipulate in your contract when the band will play and when it will take a break. You can require them to play straight through without a break, if that's what you want, but be prepared to pay extra.

THE PHOTOGRAPHER

"I hated my wedding photos. The photographer did not get the family group shots that we wanted!" Meet with the photographer ahead of time and

make sure your contract stipulates whether you want formal shots, candids, or a mix. Provide him or her with a list of people (in groups, if possible) to be photographed. Ask a friend or your wedding consultant to work with the photographer on your wedding day to make sure these shots are taken.

Tips for Disaster-Proofing Your Wedding

- Deal with reputable businesses.
- Interview everyone thoroughly.
- Prepay as little as possible. One-third to one-half of the total amount is normal procedure. Final payment is expected just before the wedding. Ask if deposits are refundable and under what circumstances.
- Pay by credit card wherever possible. If there is a dispute about a bill, the credit card company will withhold payment until it is resolved. If a caterer or bridal salon suddenly goes out of business right before your wedding, your money will not disappear as it would if you paid by check or debit card.
- Insist on contracts. They can protect you. Contracts should include what goods or services are to be provided and statements that your money will be refunded or another vendor will provide the service if needed. Read the fine print on extra charges and the cancellation policy.
- Periodically confirm everything by phone and in writing.
- Consider wedding insurance. Check your homeowners insurance and your service providers to see if you need extra coverage. Some companies offer special insurance in case of cancellation.
- Trust your instincts. Make sure you feel comfortable with the people you have hired to produce your wedding. It should be fun, so the people who are helping produce your day should be folks who genuinely want the day to be as perfect as they can make it.

"The photographer was so mean and pushy!" Many photographers are working on tight schedules, often trying to shoot more than one wedding. Find out before you sign the contract whether you will be your photographer's only concern. And, on the flip side, you don't want a photographer who is so slow and pokey that you miss the reception!

"The photographer who showed up was not the one we interviewed!" Large photography studios often have a stable of photographers. If you want a certain photographer, stipulate this in the contract.

"The photographer made us pay extra for our negatives!" This should be worked out in advance and put into your contract.

THE INVITATIONS

"The invitations arrived late from the printer and were mailed just a month before the wedding!" This is usually bride or groom error. Invitations should go out at least six weeks before the ceremony, so count backward from your wedding day and give yourself plenty of time to order. Rush shipping charges are an extra expense.

"We were charged for proofs of our invitations!" Determine up front that you will receive proofs of your invitations so you can make sure they are error-free.

"The invitations had a mistake in them!" Give yourself plenty of time to get errors corrected. The printer should do this at no charge.

Divorce

Whose Divorce Was It Anyway—
His, Hers, or Theirs?

*A*s fast as society creates a trend, sociologists slap a label on it. When twenty-somethings began rushing into marriage—and shortly thereafter, into quickie divorces—sociologists were quick to call this marriage-divorce cycle a trend, now officially known as "starter marriages."

These disposable marriages, usually childless and lasting less than a year, don't have much credibility, but they are barometers of our society's attitudes about marriage and divorce, say family counselors. Divorce is in the air, whether a marriage is less than a year old or has lasted for decades.

To slow the flood of litigation, which can be devastating for families, these experts argue for premarital counseling and for easier, less-expensive

> ∞ "My advice to girls: first, don't smoke—to excess; second, don't drink—to excess; third, don't marry—to excess."
> —*Mark Twain*

divorces. Some family counselors advocate a waiting period before a couple is allowed to marry. You can get married faster than you can buy a handgun in some states, they point out, and, unfortunately, some couples can be as volatile as a Saturday night special. To counter no-fault divorce, Louisiana has even instituted "contract marriage," a covenant that can only be broken in cases of adultery, abuse, or incest.

> ∞ "What do you call your husband's ex? I call her the practice wife."
> —A happily married second wife

But in all this talk about marriage and divorce, one important issue is left out. What about etiquette? Here are some questions I hear frequently:

- Is it right to expect Mom and Dad to pay for a big wedding when the newlyweds may split up within a year?
- There were no children, so why can't the bride have another big wedding? After all, this time she's found the right guy.
- Can't the bride wear white once again, because this time it counts and the first marriage didn't?
- What about the repeat bride whose groom, a first-timer, wants to have a big wedding?

Fortunately society no longer forces people to remain in unhappy marriages, but—call me old-fashioned—I think etiquette is right: one big wedding with all the trimmings per bride, please. And one big wedding gift per guest. No more of this "the first time didn't count."

IF THE BRIDE HAS BEEN MARRIED

Etiquette and equality of the sexes have been duking it out—politely, of course—ever since women decided they could open doors for themselves. In business situations, equality seems to be winning. Women now open doors for men, guys now get their own coffee, and whoever entered the elevator last gets off first.

But when it comes to society, the tradition concerning weddings has been discriminatory. The size and the trappings of the ceremony depended on the bride's premarital status. If she was a first-time bride, she could have as big a wedding as she wanted, with all the white-satin frills her parents could afford, no matter what her groom's nuptial history is. If she was a divorcée or a widow, she was told to have a small, quiet ceremony; keep her children out of sight; and never, ever dream of wearing a virginal white gown.

> ∞ "Happy 54th birthday to my third and best husband, Larry, from Sue."
> —*Garrison Keillor,* Prairie Home Companion

And many a first-time groom feels cheated when he learns that society frowns on a big blow-out when his bride-to-be has promised to love and honor someone else at least once or twice before. How is he ever going to get that gas grill, the preferred wedding present for two out of three grooms?

Thank goodness, times have changed. A bride can have a tasteful wedding whether this is her second time or her fourth—but who's counting?

No, the Groom Is the Divorced One

It's unfair, but a groom's marital track record is not considered when we talk weddings. If the bride is a first-timer, society traditionally has allowed her to have the most elaborate of weddings—even if she is the second or third Mrs. James Eustice Snooty III.

Grooms today often take a more active role in their weddings than their fathers and grandfathers did. Many a groom who has been married before prefers to have a simpler ceremony, often in a romantic location outside a church. But if he and his bride choose, a more elaborate ceremony is acceptable.

> ∞ "I think every woman is entitled to a middle husband she can forget."
> —*Adela Rogers St. John*

THEIR PARENTS ARE SPLIT

Whether they are amicable or angry, divorced parents create problems for a bride and groom. There are the logistical quandaries, such as who sits where, but there are emotional ones as well. A bride or groom may see the wedding as a fantasy time when, for one magical moment, their parents are together again and their broken families become the complete ones they once knew.

That isn't realistic. Wedding preparations can put so much pressure on families that even parents on the best of terms can disagree. An adult child's wedding inadvertently may be a cruel reminder of a couple's marital failure after they had begun their married lives together with love and hope.

For parents who don't get along, a child's wedding can be a time to wound their former partners. Too many brides and grooms are held hostage by parental blackmail. "If you don't do what I want," says the parent, "I won't [choose one of the following]:

- pay for the wedding."
- come to the wedding."
- ever speak to you again."
- all of the above

It's easy to say that parents should be adults about all of this. Their child is asking them to be civil to each other for only forty-eight hours or so. But does this happen? *No-o-o.* Of all the problems facing couples planning a wedding, this parental animosity is the prime cloud dampening their happiness.

Couples with divorced parents may be able to avoid much of this agony by asking their parents individually ahead of time to set their feelings and anger aside for just one day. At the same time, these brides and grooms should recognize how difficult this may be for their parents by reassuring them that they will not be asked to pose together for photographs, sit together, or dance with each other. Details should be worked out ahead of time so that everyone knows exactly what to expect.

This approach may not work for everyone, but most parents are often willing to put their children's happiness first if asked.

> "All husbands are alike, but they have different faces so you can tell them apart."
> —Anonymous

Divorce and Religion

Answering Your Questions

*J*ust as different faiths have different guidelines for marriage, most have different procedures and requirements for subsequent marriages. You may need special permission to marry again.

Below are some general guidelines, but contact your officiant for details regarding your faith.

Questions to Ask Your Officiant

- Is a civil divorce sufficient or are there additional requirements we must meet such as an annulment?
- Do we need formal or informal religious approval?
- May we write our own vows or personalize the service in any way?
- May our children be part of the ceremony?
- Must our children meet with the officiant beforehand?

- Are there any restrictions on our attire or the number of attendants we have?
- Are there any restrictions on the music we use?
- Are there any restrictions on the kinds of decorations in the church?
- May we have more than one officiant?
- Is a mixed marriage allowed?

 ## Remarriage and the Catholic Church

In the Roman Catholic Church, marriage is a sacrament and the wedding must take place in a church. Couples who want to be married in the Catholic Church must show proof of Catholic baptism. During the "prenuptial investigation," the couple is asked if they are free to marry and if they are entering marriage freely. Couples also are required to take a premarital counseling course.

Many dioceses allow Catholics to marry non-Catholics (Protestants or Jews) in the church. The ceremony is a simple one, without the usual Nuptial mass.

The Catholic Church does not recognize civil divorce. Catholics who wish to marry non-Catholics or other Catholics who have been divorced must ask for special dispensation (or permission) and the partner's first marriage has to be nullified by a church tribunal.

Catholics should turn to their priests for guidance on this issue.

Engagements

First Things First

You're finally engaged. Now what do you do?

IF THE BRIDE OR GROOM HAS BEEN MARRIED

In the past, etiquette required the man to ask the bride's father for her hand in marriage. But it seems silly to have the suiter ask for his beloved's parents' permission to marry her when she is an adult woman with a career, children, and a mortgage. Asking for permission won't be necessary the second time around. You will lovingly inform both sets of parents of your decision to marry.

And if you are parents yourselves? Your children should learn of your wedding plans from you in person, if possible. Etiquette does not dictate the exact procedure, but you know your family dynamics. If the relationships are positive, the two of you can inform your sets of children together. If not or if the children are very young, each of you may share the news with your own brood first.

In some cases, you may wish to enlist your ex-spouse's cooperation in telling your children. Tip him or her off ahead of time so that questions from the kids may be dealt with consistently by both parents.

Sometimes children see a parent's remarriage as their losing a parent instead of gaining a stepparent. You may find that seeking the advice of a trusted counselor or a clergy person beforehand is helpful.

And then there are the kids who are so eager for their single parents to remarry that they constantly try to set them up. One couple became engaged after his young son asked when "Sally" would become his real stepmother. Another couple decided the time had come to marry when, during an outing to a nice restaurant, her young daughter sighed and said, "Isn't this romantic? Just the three of us."

> ∞ "I am not in favor of long engagements. They give people the opportunity of finding out each other's character before the marriage, which I think is never advisable."
> —*Oscar Wilde*

What About My Ex?

Your ex-spouse should be one of the first to hear of your news so that he or she is able to help deal with questions from your children. But be thoughtful of your ex's feelings, even if your relationship is amicable. Although you may no longer have feelings for one another, realizing the man or woman you once loved is marrying someone else can cause a poignant pang of regret at the least.

 Tacky, Tacky, Tacky

Announcing your engagement before your divorce is final.

And watch your timing. One woman got the news of her ex-husband's engagement when he picked the kids up for the weekend. She appreciated his thoughtfulness and had time to adjust to the painful news sans children.

And if you do not communicate? A short note is the courteous thing to do.

∞ "For I'm not so old and I'm not so plain, and I'm quite prepared to marry again."
—W. S. Gilbert

A bride writes: I get along well with my fiancé's children, but he and his ex-wife are barely on speaking terms. Should he tell her of our wedding plans or should we just let her learn about our engagement through the children? — STEPMOM-TO-BE

DEAR STEPMOM: The ex-wife needs to be told of your plans, especially if the children are expected to participate or attend the ceremony. It is also a courteous gesture and shows he respects her as the mother of his children.

IF THE PARENTS ARE DIVORCED

Many couples think that asking for the bride's hand is a wonderful, old-fashioned tradition they wish to follow, even if they have lived together. And the bride's parents being divorced does not prevent the suitor from asking permission to marry his sweetheart.

If her father has been her support throughout her childhood, the groom-to-be should ask the bride's father, but it would be a lovely gesture for the groom-to-be to ask her mother, particularly if she raised the young woman. He may even wish to include the stepfather as well, particularly if his fiancé considers him to be her "real" dad.

The couple then tells the future groom's parents. If his parents are divorced, the parent with whom he spent his childhood hears the news first.

Of course, if the bride thinks this is a hopelessly old-fashioned custom or if her family does not approve of the groom, he should drop the idea.

Who Calls Whom?

After the parents have been told that their children are engaged to be married, it is a traditional courtesy for the groom's father to make a welcoming call of congratulations to the bride's parents. If the groom's parents are divorced, then the parent with whom the future bridegroom grew up does the honors. If the bride's parents are divorced, the father of the groom calls both of her parents.

Of course, this is a social nicety that is frequently overlooked these days, so no one should stand on ceremony. For example, there is nothing wrong with the bride's mother calling the groom's mother to share her excitement about the wedding.

∞ "To make sure we got things our way, we didn't tell our folks until four days before the wedding. It gave our mothers long enough to have their hair done, but not long enough to get in our hair."
—*Dianna Edwards,*
Atlanta bride

ENGAGEMENT ANNOUNCEMENT PARTIES

Engagement announcement parties are not the grand affairs they once were. Most couples prefer to put the money toward their wedding instead. But if one is held, the parents of the bride usually are hosts, or the party may be given by the groom's parents or the couple's friends.

Guests include the bride and groom and both families. A larger party might include the wedding attendants and their spouses and close friends. It can be as simple as a backyard picnic at the bride's home or as elegant as a seated dinner in a private club. It is usually mentioned in the newspaper announcement of the engagement. (Please see Newspaper Announcements.)

The father of the bride offers a toast to his daughter and her fiancé, who then responds with a toast to the bride. Other toasts follow.

An engagement party is a festive start to the activities leading up to the marriage and is a good way for the families to become acquainted. (Please see Seating for information about seating divorced families at engagement dinners.)

Engagement parties typically are not held for second weddings, but a quiet dinner hosted by the couple for their parents and/or children is a good way to become better acquainted.

Escorting the Bride

*W*alking down the aisle isn't a stroll in the park for brides who have more than one "father" in their lives. A simple rite takes on enormous importance for brides who want to honor both their natural fathers and the stepfathers with whom they grew up.

IF THE BRIDE'S PARENTS ARE DIVORCED

One of the few functions of the father of the first-time bride, other than paying the bills, is escorting his daughter down the aisle and, in some ceremonies, giving her away. This is his prerogative, although a bride is perfectly free to ask another close relative or friend to do the honors if circumstances warrant it. It is correct for the bride to be escorted by her brother, uncle or grandfather, an older son, her mother, even her stepfather. In many cases, the bride may feel closer to her step-father because she grew up in his home.

A Family Affair

In traditional Jewish weddings, both parents escort the bride down the aisle. Many non-Jewish brides are borrowing this lovely tradition, which is perfectly acceptable even in cases of divorce. But a bride should make sure that her church allows this and that her parents are comfortable with it.

"Giving Away" the Bride

In Protestant ceremonies, when the officiant asked, "Who giveth this woman?" the father of the bride's traditional answer was "I do." Then everyone's consciousness was raised, and that answer became, "Her mother and I." Even though a bride's parents are divorced, the father may still use this language.

In Catholic weddings, the church ascertains before the ceremony that a man and a woman are entering matrimony freely. Therefore, the bride is not "given away," but it is traditional for her father to escort her down the aisle.

A bride writes: My father has never been there for me and never will be. I have no stepfather, so who walks me down the aisle? Does it have to be a man?
—FATHERLESS BRIDE

✍ Wisdom from a Bride

"When you come from a messy divorce, when the father gives his daughter away and he is asked, 'Who gives this bride away?' The answer should be, 'Her family and I.' I think this makes it very cordial for all involved."

DEAR BRIDE: No, it does not have to be a man. It may be your mother or anyone important in your life. You may also walk alone, if you choose.

A bride writes: My mother and father have been divorced for three years. I never got along with my father, and he never showed much interest in me as a child. I am a young bride (twenty) so I would like to be "given away," but I prefer that my mother does it. What is the proper way of doing this? Do we hold hands, arms? —MAMA'S GIRL

DEAR MAMA'S GIRL: It would be lovely for you to have your mother walk you down the aisle and "give" you away. You two would look terrific linking arms or holding hands on your stroll.

A bride writes: After my mom and dad divorced when I was two, she and I lived with my grandparents. Although my father remarried, my mother never did, and my grandpa was a father to me. Three years ago, my mother and father remarried! I am confused. I want my father to walk me down the aisle, but I also want my grandpa. Would it be wrong to have both of them do it? —TORN IN HALF

DEAR TORN: Traditionally, it has been the father's place at his daughter's side, but why not have both your beloved grandfather and your father escort you?

A bride writes: My parents divorced when I was a baby, and my mother remarried. I never had much of a relationship with my father until I was a teenager, and most people don't realize that my stepfather is not my real dad. My father and I see each other on special occasions, but we don't have a real relationship. My fiancé says "no" to my walking down the aisle alone. I thought about asking a grandfather, but which one? My mother's father or my stepfather's father? —UNESCORTED

Dear Unescorted: Don't bring your grandfathers into this. You have enough men in your life as it is.

Traditionally, it has been a father's honored prerogative to escort his daughter down the aisle. Perhaps the true test here would be to ask yourself which man do you think of as your father in your heart of hearts. Then ask your "real" dad.

A bride writes: My father cannot attend my wedding. I have two younger brothers, twenty-two and eighteen, whom I love dearly. I also am very fortunate to have a terrific stepfather, Bill. Who should give me away? I do not want to pick between my brothers and my stepfather. I would love for my brothers to walk me down the aisle, one on either side. Could my brothers walk me to Bill, or Bill to my brothers? What would be proper? We already have seven groomsmen and two ushers. —Brotherly Love

Dear Brotherly: Having your brothers hand you off to your stepfather may look as though you were the baton in a relay race, but it also can be seen as a sweetly sentimental gesture if you can work out the logistics so that everything proceeds smoothly.

Since your fiancé has no room for your brothers on his side, have them walk down the aisle and stand on your side. Your stepfather would then escort you to stand beside your bridegroom. When everyone exits, your brothers could either pair up with the groomsmen or walk together. Your wedding consultant can help work this out.

A mother of the bride writes: I have been divorced from my daughter's father for twenty years. She has not had any dealings with him since she was sixteen. I am sponsoring a large and rather lavish wedding for her. I would like to walk her down the aisle and give her away. I feel since I have raised and cared dearly for her that it should be my right! But nowhere in any of the wedding etiquette books that I have read has this been brought up. Is this unheard of? Which side would I walk on? Does it make a difference? What type of attire should I wear? She has chosen a traditional gown with a long train and veil. Her attendants will be in black and white, with red roses to bring in color. —MICHIGAN MOTHER

DEAR MOTHER: It's a lovely idea, and your daughter should be honored to have you walk with her. She would take your right arm, so that will put her next to her fiancé.

You should choose your attire according to the formality of the wedding, following the guidelines for the mother of the bride. If the wedding is formal or ultraformal, you would wear a long dress. If it is semiformal, your dress can be tea-length or shorter. You would wear gloves and flowers.

As for color, don't give a thought to black or bright red. But you may wish to play upon some reddish hues to complement the roses the bridesmaids will carry.

A bride writes: My parents divorced when I was just a baby. My mother remarried, and my stepfather has become a wonderful dad to me. I am very close to my natural father as well and am devastated to think that I would have to pick one over the other to walk me down the aisle. Since I love my real father and my stepfather dearly, how can I have them both be a part of the day without any hurt feelings? —MY TWO DADS

DEAR TWO DADS: This is a puzzle that only you can answer because it all depends on your relationship with your fathers. More than one bride has tried to answer this question by asking one dad to walk her halfway down the aisle before handing her off to the other, but that can easily seemed contrived instead of sweet. Others have asked both dads to walk with them. Neither of these works unless both fathers are generous, understanding, and comfortable with the other's role in your life. If not, then I think the honor goes to your natural father. Of course, you could always flip a coin.

A mother of the bride writes: My daughter needs some help on which father does what. Lisa's stepfather and I will be paying for and hosting her wedding. She has lived with me and her stepfather since she was five. Her natural father lives in another state. She has good relationships with both men. Should her stepfather or her natural father walk her down the aisle? Of course, I feel her stepfather should do the honors since he not only raised her but also provided college, a car, and so forth. Lisa is not sure what she should do, only that she doesn't want to hurt either man. Is there some way to include both of them? Who "gives her away"? How does Lisa tell the father who will not walk her down the aisle that the other father has the honor? How should the wedding invitations and announcements be worded? —LISA'S MOM

DEAR MOM: Some brides compromise by having both "dads" escort them or having one man walk with her halfway down the aisle and handing her off to the other "dad." Both then give her away by saying, "Her family and I do" in unison.

Another option is asking her natural father to participate in the receiving line at the reception. But depending on your circumstances, those may not be workable.

Only Lisa can decide who has been a true father to her. Her stepfather has selflessly given her love and shelter over the years, but perhaps she feels that her father has missed out on her life and she wants him to share this part of it. It is up to her.

As for the invitations, they should be issued in your husband's and your names. (Please see Invitations and Announcements.)

IF THE BRIDE IS MARRYING FOR THE SECOND TIME

A woman who is marrying for the second time may have an escort— her father, mother, son, brother, or grandfather—down the aisle. What seems rather silly is the tradition of being "given away." That tradition of innocence belongs to first-time brides in the first blush of youth. However, if it is important to the bride and her family, the tradition may be included. If your clergy person allows it, you may consider using substitute language, such as "Who brings this woman to this marriage?"

A bride writes: This will be my second wedding. I eloped on my first marriage, denying my father the walk down the aisle. I have a nine-year-old son. Would it be more correct to walk unescorted? —SECOND TIME AROUND

DEAR SECOND: Just because you eloped the first time you married doesn't mean your father can't escort you down the aisle this time. If for some reason, your father is unavailable, your son would be a lovely substitute. It would be inappropriate, however, to have him "give" you away.

Going Solo

Whether they have been married before or whether their parents have been divorced, some brides find that the best solution to the question of who escorts them is to go it alone. One bride told me that walking done the aisle alone made her feel like a queen.

Feuding Parents

"My Parents Hate Each Other"

*T*he inspiration for this book came from dozens of couples who wrote asking for advice on dealing with their divorced parents. Some of their letters were heartbreaking stories of parents who used their children as pawns in power games with their ex-spouses. Their daughters and sons, all grown up and about to marry themselves, are still whipsawed by their parents' emotions and childish behaviors.

The game that most divorced fathers of the bride play is "Power Struggle." Usually he tempts the bride by offering to pay for all or some part of the wedding. Then he attempts to dictate what little, if any, part his former wife will play.

Divorced mothers tend to be more subtle. They play the "Guilt Game." Their line is "If he comes with his new wife, I cannot possibly be in the same room with that home-wrecker for five minutes. I'll just stay home." Or, "I think it's terrible that he insists on escorting you down the aisle when he never paid a penny of child support." Or even, "If you invite him to the wedding, you obviously are not thinking of my feelings."

Again, this situation calls for prewedding tact and diplomacy. The bride and groom should discuss their concerns with their parents and ask them to put aside their animosities for just one day. A smiling demeanor and gracious attitude cost nothing, yet earn priceless respect from their families and friends. Besides, the gracious former spouse leaves his or her ex wondering what's behind the smile.

A bride writes: If my mom pays for my wedding, she is going to insist that my brother give me away. When I tell her that my dad is going to give me away, she is going to throw a fit. And if my dad pays for it, he is going to insist that my mother have nothing to do with it. —CAUGHT IN THE MIDDLE

DEAR CAUGHT: Money seems to be the root of much of the evil here. You don't say how large your wedding is to be, or whether you have a job, but you should focus on these financial issues. Your mother and father are trying to control you via bribes. "If you don't have the wedding I want," they each say, "I'll take my checkbook and go home."

Why not remove the cause of their nyah, nyah, nyahing? It is the dream of many brides to have a grand—sometimes extravagant—wedding, but in the interest of family peace, scale your festivities down to something you and your fiancé can afford yourselves. This way *you* will be in control of the situation.

You can tell your parents—sweetly, of course—that you want them both at your wedding, but you are planning the affair, and that's that. If they would like to contribute financially, you would appreciate it, but that contribution does not entitle them to dictate the wedding plans.

Remind them that you don't want your wedding to be a battleground. Ask for a truce. If they are planning to ambush each other, say you are sorry and suggest that they might prefer to stay home.

A bride writes: My father and stepmother raised me, and I barely know my real mother at all. My father and stepmother are paying for most of the wedding, so my stepmother will be considered the mother of the bride. I was wondering if there was something nice that I could do for my real mother without making anyone angry. I am afraid that if I do too much for her, my father and his wife will get mad and refuse to pay for the wedding. They do not get along at all. —Too Many Moms

Dear Too Many: A mother of the bride does not have a large, on-stage role in a wedding after she takes her seat in the front row, but you can honor your mother perhaps by giving her a flower from your bouquet as you leave the church. Just so no one is left out, your groom may wish to give one to his mother and you may present another one to your stepmother. You should also have a corsage on hand for your mother to wear.

A bride writes: I'm sure this question is asked often in these times. What can I do with four sets of parents who have had acrimonious divorces and will be insufferable in the same room together? My parents are the main problem. My mother says she won't come to my wedding but will visit later to avoid my dad. (But if I had to choose, I would prefer to have my mother there.) My father, however, has made it clear that he wouldn't miss his only daughter's wedding for anything. Eloping is becoming a tempting option! I haven't seen them and their spouses in two years, partly because I avoid going "home" since I have to deal with such petty childishness as never mentioning the other parent or my plans involving the other parent. My fiancé and I are considering holding a private ceremony and inviting the family to a reception after the honeymoon. But I am thirty-five, never married, and this seems like a bit of a short change! —Daughter of Children

Dear Daughter: How heartbreaking that your parents' squabbles threaten your happiness on your wedding day. It is hard to understand parents who are so selfish that they cannot put aside their animosities long enough for their daughter to get married—about three hours!

I know you are carrying a lot of emotional baggage, but if I were you, I would tell my parents individually how I felt. I would tell them I want them at my wedding, but that I was not going to give in to their childish demands. If they were going to make a scene, they are not welcome. Then, I would go on with my plans, ignoring their attempts to make me feel guilty.

A bride writes: Beacause of a split family, I have two of everything—two moms, two dads—and the two sides do not get along! I still want to include everyone in our traditional, formal wedding. Could I have both of my mothers light a candle? Could I have both of my fathers give me away? All four raised me, and I don't want anyone left out. —SETS OF TWO

DEAR TWO: Having four parents participate in a "traditional, formal wedding" is not very traditional. Because of the ill feeling between your two families, your biological mother and father should get star billing. Your stepparents should stay in the background. However, they may stand in the receiving line. (Please see Receiving Lines for suggestions.) When the dancing begins, they should dance with their spouses (your parents) after you and your fiancé have had a turn around the dance floor.

A bride writes: My mother died when I was very young. My stepmother, who is the only mother I ever knew, will be "mother of the bride." Is this proper? She is no longer married to my father, who married a woman with whom I am barely on speaking terms. My father and I are not close, but he may offer to host the reception. How can I ask him tactfully? How should the invitations be worded? Where do I seat everyone in church? Would that change if my brother escorts me down the aisle if my father doesn't want to? What should I do if my fiancé's father (his mother is also dead) doesn't initiate a get-acquainted meeting with my family? —NO FAMILY TREE

DEAR FAMILY: You need to sit down with your papa and ask him if he will escort you and host your wedding reception. If he agrees, then the wedding invitations may be issued in his name only (although it is incorrect for the name of your father's new wife to be omitted from the invitations, given your poor relationship, her name need not appear). Your father would also escort you down the aisle. If he declines, the invitations may be issued by your brother, who may also escort you down the aisle. If your father wants to escort you but refuses to pay for the reception, you and your fiancé should consider issuing the invitations yourselves. (Please see Invitations.)

The honour of your presence
is requested at the marriage of
Miss Christine Bergen Paterson
and
Mr. Joseph Garfield Ramsey, II
[and so forth]

The seating of the mothers is not a special rite, but is a tradition that tips the guests off that the ceremony is about to begin. If you like, you may give your former stepmother, who is no relation to you now, the honor of being seated in the first row. Your father would sit with his current wife as far behind your former stepmother as you wish.

Your fiancé should prompt his father to arrange a meeting with your father in a social setting. If his father isn't comfortable with this, you and your fiancé can host a small, casual get-together. Include your new stepmother.

A bride writes: I am a twenty-three-year-old college graduate on the verge of engagement. I have worried about this problem for some time now, but as my boyfriend and I begin to discuss marriage, I am anxiety-ridden about the wed-

ding. I am an only child. My parents divorced when I was six. My mother raised me with little financial assistance from my father. He is remarried with three children. My mother died when I was eighteen, and I put myself through college. I don't expect my father to help pay for my wedding. My fiancé and I will pay for the entire thing. I don't want my father to "give" me away because I don't think he owns me. I do love him, and he will be very hurt if he does not walk me down the aisle. My mother would not want him to escort me. What do you suggest? —DIVIDED LOYALTY

DEAR DIVIDED: Many of today's brides also find the "giving away" part of the marriage ceremony distasteful. They merely eliminate it from the service.

As for walking you down the aisle, what do *you* want? Surely your deceased mother would want you to be happy. If you love your father and want him to escort you, by all means ask him.

A bride writes: My parents were divorced fifteen years ago. My stepfather took care of me for thirteen years before he and my mother divorced three years ago. Both men will be involved in the wedding. When three parents are involved— none of them married to each other!—how are the invitations worded? Where do I seat everyone? What is the best way to have a receiving line? Is it appropriate to have two men escort the bride? How do I handle the tensions that will develop that day? —COMPLETELY CONFUSED

DEAR CONFUSED: You don't. *They* do. And they handle those tensions by being sweet and charming to each other. They're all grown up, and they should be able to put their problems behind them for the twenty-four hours it takes to get the daughter they love married.

Rather than have a hodgepodge of names on the invitation, why not issue the wedding invitations in your mother's name? Your father and his wife may issue the invitation to the reception. That way, everyone gets star billing.

Your mother and her escort sit in the first row on the left. Your father and his wife may sit directly behind her—or farther back if that's too close for comfort. Your stepfather and his escort sit even farther toward the rear of the wedding site.

The best way to have a receiving line, the men in your life will agree, is to leave it for the women. Include your mother, your new mother-in-law, you, and your new husband to make the receiving line short and sweet.

Despite your loving ties, your stepfather is no longer related to you. The honor of escorting you down the aisle is your father's—unless your stepfather means more to you than your father ever did.

A bride writes: In wording my invitations, I encountered a dilemma. My mother has remarried, and the invitations were supposed to read:

Mr. and Mrs. Horace Harding
invite you to share
in the joy of the marriage
uniting her daughter . . .

 Hopeless Cases

In some cases, there are so many bad feelings that the groom or the bride should give up trying to get his or her parents to the same reception. One Chicago bride solved this problem by having just her mother and the groom's parents present at a small ceremony and reception. She then allowed her father and his new wife to host another party later, to which she wore her wedding finery.

Unfortunately, the invitations read their *daughter. I was willing to accept the invitations, but at my mother's insistence—and a good deal of expense—we re-ordered. Was this necessary?* —DAUGHTER AND STEP-DAUGHTER

DEAR DAUGHTER: No, the typographical mistake was socially correct. "Their daughter" is correct—if you were raised by your mother and her husband or your relationship with your stepfather is amicable.

A bride writes: My fiancé and I want to have a formal wedding, but there is a sticky bit. His father and mother were divorced when he was very young, and his mother remarried. When he was sixteen, she divorced his stepfather, with whom he continued to live. Then his stepfather remarried. Now his mother will have nothing to do with the stepfather. What do we do about his real father? About his mother and her new husband? About his stepparents? (We want them to be a big part of the ceremony.) And last, what about my parents, who are going through a nasty divorce? When they are in the same room it is like going to a boxing match. Who stands in the receiving line? What can I do to have them be nice to each other? —TOO MANY PARENTS

DEAR TOO: You can tell them to behave. Take the various warring parties aside privately and have a little chat. Ask them to put aside their differences for just twenty-four hours. Tell them you understand that they are unhappy and you are sensitive to their feelings, but this is your day, and you and your fiancé deserve to have a smooth, trouble-free wedding that you can enjoy. No bickering. No huffiness. No pouting.

Now for your other questions:

- Your fiancé's father: If they are close, your fiancé may want him to act as best man. If not, he is invited to the wedding just like any other guest and seated on the groom's side several rows back.

- His mother and her new husband: They get the seat of honor, the front right row.

- His former stepparents: They should be invited just like any other guests and seated on the groom's side of the church. The man is no longer related to your fiancé and should not be part of the ceremony unless your fiancé asks him to act as a groomsman. The new wife of your fiancé's former stepfather is not his stepmother. If your fiancé's father has remarried, his wife is your fiancé's stepmother.

- Your parents: They will have to act civilly toward one another, but your father should sit in the row behind your mother after he escorts you down the aisle, unless their divorce was particularly acrimonious. Then he is seated several rows back.

- The receiving line: Fathers are not required to stand in a receiving line. The lineup should be your mother, your new mother-in-law, you, and your new husband. Your maid of honor may bring up the end of the line.

- Family photographs are another sore spot for divorce-riddled families. I suggest that you and your fiancé pose with each family faction. Don't ask the warring parties to pose with each other.

Flowers

Petal-Powered Weddings

*U*nless the couple is paying for the wedding themselves, the families of the bride and groom share the cost of the flowers, with each side paying for certain things, such as the groom picking up the cost of the bride's bouquet. Of course, this custom may vary in different parts of the country, so everything should be discussed without making assumptions.

Flowers for a second marriage are usually less elaborate than those for a first wedding. Depending upon what best complements her attire, the bride may carry a small bouquet or wear a corsage. Flowers also are an attractive alternative to a veil.

Some churches and synagogues may have restrictions on flowers for second weddings. Ask your clergy person when you begin planning.

Flowers Purchased by the Family of the Bride
- All flowers used as decorations for the ceremony and the reception
- Bouquets and floral headpieces for the honor attendants, bridesmaids, and flower girls
- Corsages for any friends assisting at the reception
- Flowers sent to hostesses who entertained the couple

Flowers Purchased by the Family of the Groom
- The bride's bouquet
- A corsage for the bride's going-away outfit
- Corsages for the mother of the bride, the mother of the groom, the grandmothers, and other honored guests, such as aunts or sisters
- Boutonnieres for the groom, the best man, the fathers, and the groomsmen

A bride writes: My fiancé's parents are divorced and have remarried. Is it necessary to provide flowers for all of the stepparents and step-grandparents?
—Flower Child

Dear Flower: Flowers for honored guests are a nice gesture. You may even order them for an aunt or a sister, but it is not necessary to present them to a step-grandparent who your fiancé does not really know. You and your fiancé should decide whom you wish to honor. Traditionally the groom pays for these corsages.

A Visit to the Florist

Make your trip to the florist productive by doing some advance preparation.

• Visit your ceremony and reception sites to get an idea of what kinds of arrangements you will need and how large to make them. Ask the wedding guide at your wedding location for suggestions. If your florist or caterer has worked the site before, ask him or her for ideas.

• Don't overlook unusual places where flowers can have great impact: over the door of the reception site, in the ladies rest room, or draped along a stair banister or a porch railing.

• Find inspiration for flowers, bouquets, centerpieces, and decorations in magazines and books. Bring those pictures during your first visit. It's easier to show the florist what you want than trying to describe it. (The same goes with wedding hairstyles for the bride's stylist.)

• Show the florist pictures of the gown and bridesmaid dresses. He or she can recommend bouquet styles and floral colors that will complement the gowns. Bring a swatch of the fabric for the bridesmaid's gown, too, if you can.

• Research flowers at the library or on the Internet to find varieties of flowers you like. Visit flower shops and farmers markets to learn about flowers and their prices.

• Ask your florist to show you photographs of what will be in season around the date of your wedding. Flowers that are in season are less expensive than flowers that have to be grown especially for your wedding. They may also hold up better than delicate greenhouse flowers. Wedding and home magazines also are good sources for creative use of in-season floral materials such as holly for winter weddings or pumpkins as "vases" at fall weddings.

• Consider using silk flowers. Many couples find silk flowers to be an affordable alternative—and they can be enjoyed for years.

Garter-Bouquet Debate

To Toss or Not to Toss?

*T*oday's brides are finally wising up—or maybe they have been to one too many weddings before they became engaged. They are dropping that tradition detested by so many single women: tossing the bridal bouquet. It's been my observation that the only single females at a reception who enjoy being herded together so they could look like idiots fighting over a handful of flowers average twelve years of age.

In the same vein, many brides feel embarrassed by a tradition that calls for them to hike up their skirts and flaunt a bit of leg so their grinning husbands can remove a useless lace garter.

Neither of these traditions is very dignified or sophisticated, so brides and grooms may skip them if they choose. By the same token, even second-time brides are perfectly free to keep the fun and games if they enjoy them.

A bride writes: My fiancé and I have been having a major discussion—OK, a fight—about this whole garter-bouquet mess. He wants to go whole-hog, including having the guy who catches the garter put it on bouquet-catcher's leg. I think the whole idea is tacky. Blake says he wants a "touch of eroticism" at our reception and the guy should "get a reward" for catching the garter. I am truly disgusted at that. What do you think? Please don't tell me to just "lighten up." —GROSSED-OUT BRIDE

DEAR GROSSED-OUT: I think you are very considerate of your unmarried friends not to single them out. It's even less appropriate to force a woman to let a strange man touch her in an intimate way, particularly with the crowd cheering (leering?). Tell Blake to save his "touch of eroticism" for the honeymoon.

Gifts

The Gift Registry

One of the most charming perks of being an engaged couple is receiving gifts. For weeks before the wedding, it is as if every day is Christmas with mysterious boxes arriving on the doorstep. Even the couple who has meticulously registered for everything from forks to fondue pots to frying pans will find themselves surprised and delighted by the thoughtfulness and originality of family and friends.

The bridal registry originally was considered to be an efficient way to help couples furnish their new homes with expensive china, silver, and crystal. The registry was meant to serve as a guide to bewildered guests, not as a method for the bride and groom to dictate what they want.

Instead of sterling silver and porcelain china, today's couples are more likely to register for household items that better suit their more casual lifestyles, but some couples overstep the bounds of propriety.

Their wedding invitations include lists of the stores where they are registered or stipulate that money is the gift of choice. Some couples even register for money in the form of stocks and bonds or "invite" guests to contribute to funds for a honeymoon or new home.

And then, on the other end of the spectrum, are the couples already blessed with an abundance of worldly goods. "Instead of wedding gifts," they say, "please donate to our favorite charity." Their grand, unselfish gesture lets others less fortunate benefit from their wedding day, yet it also robs guests of the opportunity to choose a gift for the couple.

When a gift giver is told what the "gift" will be, the gift is no longer an offering but becomes the price of admission to a wedding reception. Wedding gifts symbolize joy and love from family and friends during this special time in a couple's lives. Those wonderfully wrapped surprises are more than just household articles intended to help the bride and groom set up their new home together. Each and every gift is an expression of affection and best wishes from the giver. It is love and caring wrapped up with a bow.

As I have often said, gifts should be freely given, not wrung out of guests in a form of social blackmail. The proper attitude for the bride and groom is not "this is what we want and don't bother giving us anything else," but "how wonderful for you to remember us at this special time in our lives."

*A bride writes: I am a forty-year-old bride, and my fiancé and I will be combining two households. We would like people to consider donating to our church or another charity we support. How can we word this on an enclosure card within the invitation? —*WANTS TO GIVE

DEAR WANTS: While your intentions are admirable, the idea could come across as tacky. It is considered impolite to tell people what to give you because 1) it presupposes that you are getting a gift, and 2) it

> ∞ "The manner in which it is given is worth more than the gift."
>
> —*Pierre Corneille*

negates the whole idea of a gift, which is something freely given. When a guest is told exactly what to give, it becomes a sort of bridal extortion.

Instead, you can achieve your wishes more subtly. Do not register at any department stores. Enlist your family to let people know that nothing would make you happier than a donation to your favorite charity. Tell people who ask you the same thing. This is more trouble, but it is a much more gracious approach.

TO REGISTER OR NOT TO REGISTER?

For decades, couples marrying again were considered tacky if they registered for gifts. The rule was that gifts were de rigueur only when the bride married for the first time. Since a woman usually kept the wedding gifts if she divorced, the rule applied only to brides, not grooms. A groom could marry as frequently as the law allowed and guests were still expected to come bearing gifts if his subsequent bride had never married. Most guests knew that gifts were not expected at second weddings.

But times have changed. A woman is more likely to be divorced or to marry later in life. With divorce rates so high, more men and women are entering multiple marriages. Should a second-time bride

 Tacky, Tacky, Tacky

A wedding guest was hurt and puzzled when she received a note thanking her for her wedding gift and explaining that, since they had already had everything they needed, the newlyweds were donating her gift to charity. "Didn't they like it?" she wondered sadly. "Wasn't it nice enough for them?"

register to ensure she and her groom receive what they want or what is useful?

It depends. The problem for most couples is not how to fill up a house but what to do with all of their stuff. But that's not true for everyone. The bride or groom may have lost household furnishings in a divorce, and they are truly starting over in creating a home together. Or maybe they want to register for new china so they won't have to set their breakfast table with reminders of a former marriage.

Many couples have new sets of friends who may not even remember the prior marriages. In reality, many guests are going to give gifts because they want to commemorate the occasion.

It's time to change the rules. No, this change won't make it OK for greedy couples to force their friends and families into upgrading their home furnishings, but it will allow some latitude for today's multiple marriages. Here's the new rule: one gift per guest (or couple).

So, register if you wish. We won't make snide remarks. Just don't expect a lavish gift from a guest who contributed to your last marriage.

A bride writes: Is it proper to have a bridal registry for a second wedding?
—Second-Time Bride

Dear Second: Yes, it is permissible. There will always be guests who wish to honor the newlyweds. The second-time bride, however, should not expect as many gifts as she got the first time around, and she should

Tacky, Tacky, Tacky

An Atlanta millionaire, marrying for the fourth time, registered on-line for wedding gifts. What did Mr. and Mrs. Got-Rocks want? Waterford crystal wineglasses from Neiman Marcus and a melon scoop from Williams-Sonoma. When you have that much money and have been married that many times, please forgo the gift registry. This couple could afford a boatload of Waterford.

only mention the registry if asked. Brides, whether on their first marriage or their third, should also select gifts in a variety of price ranges.

A bride writes: My fiancé and I want to have monetary gifts only. We have a home and feel as though those dreaded gifts that will be duplicated will only have to be returned. Please send suggestions as to what to put onto the invitations. —Just Cash Please

Dear Cash: There is no "proper" way of requesting money in lieu of gifts. Not only is it a terribly tacky thing to do, but it is also insulting. By asking for money—in other words, *demanding* what friends and relatives give them—a couple commits bridal blackmail and negates the meaning of the word *gift*. A gift is something freely given, chosen by someone who cares about you and hopes to please you. By telling that person what to give you, the "present" is no longer a gift, but blackmail. "If you want to come to my wedding, you'd better give me what I want." Your words, "dreaded gifts," reveal exactly what you think of the people you're inviting to your wedding.

By the way, guests are not obligated to give gifts at second weddings. Couples usually have established households, and wedding gifts are to help couples going out on their own for the first time. But friends and family will want to give you remembrances of your day, so please, let them choose what they wish to give.

Grooms

A Wedding Day Essential

A bride can't have a wedding without a groom, or can she? In our grandmothers' day, grooms were superfluous when it came to wedding planning. The bride and her mother took over, making all the decisions on every aspect of the wedding and reception. The groom's duties primarily consisted of showing up at the right church—on time—wearing a properly tied bow tie and black socks, not blue.

To some guys, planning a wedding should be simple. Find an officiant and just do it. None of this agonizing over beef or chicken or lilies versus lilacs for them. Chili and beer would be the ideal menu, and who cares about flowers? But let him find out that his bride is thinking of making the males in the wedding party carry canes and wear top hats and see how fast he becomes involved in the planning.

Thank goodness times have changed! From the moment he proposes, today's groom is part of the prewedding picture. Engagement photos printed in hometown newspapers, once a page of female faces only, now feature both bride and groom.

Showers frequently have coed guest lists and are planned around themes guys like so the presents are often guy stuff: tools, bottles of wine, gas grills, camping gear, and so forth. You don't see too many grooms waxing ecstatic over a complete place setting in their best china.

For many men today—and you lucky brides know who you are— the groom is no longer content to be a decorative accessory on his wedding day. This husband-to-be sees his wedding as the first step in his and his bride's long-awaited life together as husband and wife. He, like his bride, is eager to make sure that the wedding day is an expression of the love they feel for each other and for their friends and family. He wants to ensure that every aspect of the wedding day is joyous and fun.

Just what is his role, other than pledging his troth and being able to carry the bride over the threshold? The etiquette books list the items that a groom and his family are "responsible for," in other words, must pay for. But what are his other duties? How is he supposed to act? What sort of etiquette must he follow?

Why, the same as any gentleman. He stands up when ladies or older men enter the room. He has a firm, manly handshake and always opens doors for women. He even listens politely as the bride's Uncle Hugh repeats the same tired jokes.

Today's groom knows he needs monogrammed stationery for the thank-you notes he must write. He remembers to introduce people at the reception and rescues wallflowers whenever possible. He carries a clean handkerchief and never overindulges in alcoholic beverages. He even takes dancing lessons, if need be, in preparation for the moment in the spotlight at the reception.

But what the etiquette books might not reveal is that there are little touches that will endear the groom to everyone around him. He should offer to help the bride's mother as much as possible, supplying her with a legible list of his wedding guests' names and addresses, for example. Making reservations for his out-of-town family and guests is his responsibility. It goes without saying that he must be on time to all parties given in his honor, and he must not be late for the rehearsal and to the wedding.

On his wedding day, the groom makes sure that his mother has an escort to the church. At the reception, he follows the best man's first toast with a loving toast to his bride. He bids farewell to all of the parents and, later, phones his thanks. Then he makes sure that he and his bride have a *fabulous* honeymoon.

He is attentive to his bride, but he is never overly affectionate in public. He supports her as she plans the day, never whining about picking out china or reading bride magazines. And, even though he's known as a practical joker, he never, ever crams wedding cake into his bride's face or pretends to pull off her panties instead of her garter.

∞ "I didn't marry you because you were perfect. I didn't even marry you because I loved you. I married you because you gave me a promise. That promise made up for your faults. And the promise I gave you made up for mine. Two imperfect people got married, and it was the promise that made the marriage. And when our children were growing up, it wasn't a house that protected them; and it wasn't our love that protected them—it was that promise."

—The Skin of Our Teeth *by Thornton Wilder*

A bride writes: My fiancé has two middle names that he never uses. They are not even on his driver's license or passport. Instead, he uses initials. James C. D. Martin is what he wants on the wedding invitations, even though I have told him this is incorrect. When I suggested that we just use James Martin, he says he likes the C. D. because it keeps people from wondering if he has a middle name. What should I do? —NAME GAME

DEAR NAME: To be perfectly correct, you should put your fiancé's middle names on the invitation, but it's not that big of a deal. If he is embarrassed by his names, do not make him feel uncomfortable. No great Etiquette God in the sky is going to come down and smite you for using initials. The worst thing that can happen is that some elderly ladies may gossip about you, but that's a small price to pay for his happiness.

Guest List and Gift Record

Making a List and Checking It and Checking It . . .

*Y*our mom probably used an alphabetized index card file to keep track of her guests and gifts when she was married, but you may decide to keep your list in your computer. Keeping accurate records of who's coming to the wedding and who has sent a gift is essential for planning the reception and for making sure everyone is thanked properly. (Please see Thank-You Notes and Computers.)

The following information will be needed for your guest list:

- Guest's name in this order: last name, title, given name. For example: Abernathy, Mr. and Mrs. Roger D. (Annabel)
- Complete mailing address
- Names of children younger than eighteen who are invited
- Phone number
- Acceptance or regrets (to be added when the guest responds)

If you are sending
out wedding
announcements as well
as invitations, you need
to keep a separate list
for announcements.
You also probably will
receive some gifts from
people who are not
invited to the wedding.
And be sure to keep
any receipts that arrive
with gifts in case
anything must be
returned. ∞

Whether you choose a high- or low-tech method, gifts may be recorded on your guest list. The following information should be added:

- Description of gift
- Store from which it came
- Date received
- Date that thank-you note was written

In addition to this record, a short description of the gift and giver also should be recorded on the gift cards, which should be saved. Each gift card should be given a number that corresponds to a number for a guest on your card file or computer list. For example, "No. 5, candlesticks from M/Mrs. B. B. Brown" should be cross-referenced "M/Mrs. B. B. Brown" on your list. This is especially helpful for couples who receive hundreds of gifts and for making returns.

Guests

How Big Is Too Big?

*U*nfortunately, many parents use weddings as a chance to "pay back" social obligations, and the poor bride and groom find themselves greeting strangers. A second wedding is a joyous opportunity to celebrate with family and close friends, the people you love and care about—and who care about you. This time, since the bride and groom are usually paying for everything themselves, they feel free to invite whom they wish—without paying back Mom and Dad's social obligations.

"We'd both been married before," said one bride. "The best part this time was that we only invited the people who we really love. We knew they were there because they cared about us—not for the free meal."

The number of guests to invite to your second wedding depends on:

- How many friends you have
- How big your budget is
- How close you are to your father's third cousin

TEN TACKY THINGS GUESTS DO (AND HOW TO BE PREPARED)

Unfortunately, every couple knows these "guests from hell." These are the guests who:

1. **Ask if they can bring a date or an escort.** Your answer is "I'm terribly sorry, but our guest list has been set, and we cannot include any extras." You need not go into details. It's none of Tacky Guest's business. Stand your ground when Tacky Guest offers to pay for his or her escort. A wedding is not a singles party.

2. **Show up with a date or an escort anyway.** This time, Tacky Guest has outflanked you, and there is nothing you can do about it except smile coldly when introduced. After the wedding, you can decide if this is a friendship worth keeping.

3. **Assume their little darlings are invited to the wedding.** Try to foil these Tacky Guests by having Mom or an aunt call before the wedding and remind them that children are not invited. As a last resort,

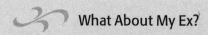 **What About My Ex?**

Ex-spouses are no longer required company, so there's no need to include these reminders of the past. Invite a former spouse only if your divorce is very ancient history and the three of you are *very* good friends. The same goes for other family members from a past marriage. Be sure your fiancé signs off on this before sending the invitations. After all, how would *you* feel if your betrothed wanted to invite his or her ex?

make a stand at the church door by having ushers shuffle the little ones off into a nursery.

4. **Bring presents to the reception.** Gifts should be sent to the home of the bride or to the address on the invitation. There are too many chances that a gift could be lost or stolen at the reception. There also is an excellent chance that the card will be misplaced, and the couple will not know whom to thank. But this has become accepted practice as our society has become more mobile. The smart bride and groom ask someone to be in charge of taping cards to gifts and removing the packages after the reception.

5. **Switch place cards at the reception dinner.** You both work for hours trying to arrange the seating so your families will get to know each other and have fun together. Some thoughtless Tacky Guest ruins all your hard work by rearranging the cards because she didn't like where she was to be seated. Avoid this problem by assigning people to tables and then letting them arrange themselves at their tables. Realize that weddings are family reunion times, and your guests will want to visit with relatives they haven't seen in a while.

6. **Pout in the corner at the reception.** One of the duties of Polite Guest is being friendly and mingling with your other guests. While some guests are relatives-who-must-be-invited, others are there because you genuinely want them to share the most important day of your life. Because you know and care about them, you also want them to know each other.

7. **Become drunk and obnoxious.** Make sure the wait staff is well-trained in recognizing when Tacky Guest has had too much to drink and in knowing how to handle the problem. Most caterers are very aware of their liability if guests are allowed to overindulge.

8. **Enjoy the reception and then leave—without ever having spoken to the bride or groom.** Avoid this by having a receiving line at the reception so that you have a chance to greet everyone. Brides and

grooms who do not have receiving lines, even abbreviated ones, have only themselves to blame for this faux pas. Guests cannot be expected to chase you around the room to say hello.

9. **Do not respond to your invitation.** These people are the rudest of the rude. You and your mother have my permission to call Tacky Guest and embarrass him or her by being sweetly solicitous. "My dear, when I did not hear from you in a timely fashion, I was afraid some terrible ailment had befallen you. Perhaps your writing hand was broken or you had lost your voice." You needn't lay it on so thick, but you get the picture.

10. **Say "yes!" and then are no-shows.** The only excuses are accidents, illnesses, or death. Wedding invitations should not be shrugged off lightly if something more appealing comes along.

WHAT ABOUT KIDS?

While some couples can't imagine a wedding that doesn't include the children, not every bride and groom welcome little ones as guests at their wedding. But be forewarned. That decision can cause problems with family and friends, who simply cannot understand why a couple would not want the little dears whining so adorably throughout the ceremony or dashing headlong among formally dressed guests at the evening reception.

How can we get parents to leave their children at home? The answer is don't invite them. Adults with any social savvy will realize

Tacky, Tacky, Tacky

Please don't put "Adults-only reception" on your invitations. Just because you are afraid some of your guests will be tacky doesn't allow you to be.

that their children are not included when the little ones' names are not on the wedding invitation.

For the socially inept parent, the bride or groom may have to be more obvious, saying "We're so sorry that we cannot include little Angelique and little Wally, but we decided to make this a party for adults only." Smart couples will enlist their moms to help spread the word.

For couples who do want to include youngsters, a few tips:

• Consider the time of day. Kids do better at daytime weddings, while evening weddings conflict with bedtime.

• Think about the children when planning the reception. A buffet might be more "kid-friendly" than a lengthy seated dinner, when even adults are apt to fidget.

• Hire a teenager to be in charge of the children at the reception. This "babysitter" can make sure the younger set gets plenty of time on the dance floor to work off energy.

*A bride writes: It's important to us that our young nieces and nephews share our wedding day, so we have asked all of them to be in our wedding. No other children have been invited. I've already been asked by guests if I've hired any sitters. I can't believe that people actually expect me to arrange for sitters for their kids, who are not invited! —*No Kidding

Dear No Kidding: Many brides have to resort to hiring a sitter to take care of the kids who show up at the door of the church with their doting parents. The ushers are instructed to detour these offspring of thoughtless people to the nursery.

A bride vents: I'm tired of people saying that I'm selfish because I choose not to have other people's children at my wedding. If people knew how to make their children behave, that would be one thing, but many parents just let them

run wild. I'm not paying thousands of dollars for a wedding reception only to have kids waste food and overrun the dance floor. —ADULTS ONLY

DEAR ADULTS ONLY: I couldn't agree with you more. "Wouldn't it be nice," a harried mom told me recently, "if kids skipped childhood and went from being cuddly babies to twenty-one year olds?" We laughed at the idea. No parent wants to miss a moment of childhood, but some days . . .

It would be great if children were better behaved, but we live in permissive times. Unfortunately many parents were reared without learning manners themselves, so how can they pass this valuable lesson along to their offspring? Just promise me that when *your* babies come along, you will remember your words.

Honeymoons

"We're Out of Here!"

$\mathcal{A}$ honeymoon for second-timers? Of course! And as romantic and fun as you can afford. But second-time couples have honeymoon complications most first-timers never consider.

CHILDREN

Should they come along on the honeymoon? Sometimes it's hard for couples to remember that they should be newlyweds first and a mom or dad second. Newlyweds need to spend some private "couple time" together. But that's not always possible as a bride who made a wonderful stepmother found out. "When my husband and I were married, his ex-wife refused to keep his children after our wedding, and we had no one to leave them with. So the five of us spent our wedding night together. Not very romantic, but a lot of fun."

If the children must be included, a half-and-half honeymoon may be the answer. The first half is off limits to the children, who join their parents for the second half. If schedules won't permit this, the "children's honeymoon" is planned later, with calendars marked so the youngsters have something to look forward to. Look for resorts or cruises with lots of planned activities for the kids, so there is plenty of "couple time."

Memories

Planning a repeat honeymoon to a romantic spot once shared with a former spouse is a bad idea. While the returnee may have the best of intentions, who wants a honeymoon peopled with ghosts? It's too easy to revive past loves and disappointments. The world is a big place. Find some spot that can be special for the two of you.

In-Laws

Whose Wedding—Yours or Theirs?

*I*t's often said that a wedding is more than the union of two people who wish to spend their lives together—it's the joining of two families. On your wedding day, you will be gaining more than just a spouse. You also will be getting another set of relatives—parents and brothers and sisters, plus or minus a few nieces and nephews.

These folks will become almost as important to you as your own family, for richer, for poorer and in sickness and in health. A good relationship with your in-laws will give you a firmer foundation for your own marriage.

That relationship may have begun when the two of you were dating. It may have begun when you became engaged. But no matter how long you have known your future in-laws, the pressures and stresses of planning a wedding can strain even the best of relationships.

Many a bride has told me that she doesn't "feel close" to her fiancé's sisters and doesn't want them as her bridesmaids. This bride can't understand why her fiancé's family is furious and the sisters are hurt.

Other couples write that their mothers-in-law want to impose their thoughts on how the wedding should be held. "It's my day" or "I'm paying for it," these brides say. "I want to do it my way." I know a salon owner who has a special name for this bride: *Bridezilla.*

Still other couples are angry when the parents of their betrothed do not step forward to offer to help with the expenses. They want to know if there is some way—very correct, of course—to shame or force the groom's family into paying for the wedding or get the bride's family to spend more.

But other couples welcome suggestions, turning "my way" into "our way." This couple sees the big picture. They understand that their wedding day is merely the prelude to a married life that will be much happier if the families get along well together. They know that their attitude during this stressful time is the key to future relations.

So how do you do it? I know one bride who telephoned her future mother-in-law almost daily to talk about the wedding plans. The mother-in-law recently lost her husband, and those calls meant so much to her. By reaching out to her future mother-in-law, this bride has so endeared herself to the rest of the groom's extended family that she could have turned cartwheels down the aisle and everyone would have thought it was great.

But what about couples faced with the proverbial "mother-in-law from hell" or a mother who has serious behavioral or substance abuse problems? What about controlling fathers with a tight grip on the purse strings? And when you factor in divorce . . . how do we cope with that?

You do your best. The gracious bride and groom will find ways to include each other's families. They will listen to wedding ideas from the other side of the aisle and try to incorporate them when they can.

They will stick to their budget and forgo planning a wedding beyond their means. They may have to smile through gritted teeth as they listen to complaints about their decisions, but their ability to keep cool is essential to a joyous wedding day and a blissful married life—because those "suggestions" and complaints are not going to end with the wedding. These couples know that their wedding day is merely the first day of their new life with each other—and their new families.

A bride writes: My mother and I attended a bridal show, and one of the speakers discussed the topic of what to call your husband's mother after you are married. My mother asked me what I was going to call my husband's mother. My mother has asked me this question twice. My fiancé is very close to his mother, being her only son. I know he would be very hurt if I did not call her "Mom." I do not want to hurt my mother's or husband's feelings. What should I do? —HER MOTHER'S DAUGHTER

DEAR DAUGHTER: What do you call your fiancé's mother now? Mrs. Lastname? Or are you on a first-name basis? Does she have a nickname that her grandchildren call her? What do her sons-in-law call her?

This is a very personal issue. I, for one, would have felt uncomfortable calling my dear mother-in-law, "Mom." I called her Nanny, as her grandchildren did. Sometimes I used her first name, but Nanny just seemed to fit best as a term of endearment.

Why don't you discuss this alone with your future mother-in-law? Tell her your concerns and ask her, "What do you want me to call you?" Ask her if she has a nickname she would like for you to use. Your future mother-in-law will appreciate your candor and your efforts to be a good daughter-in-law. Then tell your fiancé of your mutual decision.

> "Marriage is a great institution—no family should be without it."
> —*Bob Hope*

A bride writes: My wedding is weeks away, and I still have so much to do. My fiancé and I are paying for the entire wedding, so I am making most of *the decorations myself—centerpieces, pew bows, even flower girl accessories— because we are trying to keep costs down. My future mother-in-law has absolutely no clue as to how little time I have. She keeps inviting us to go "do things" with her—craft projects, shopping, cooking. We have explained that we are simply too busy now, but we'll be available after the wedding. Whenever we try to explain, she complains about how aloof and unfriendly I am, yet she doesn't want to help with the wedding projects. It's as if she doesn't want to acknowledge the amount of work that we are putting into this wedding. How do I get her to understand? —*FRUSTRATED BRIDE

DEAR FRUSTRATED: It sounds as if you are doing all the right things— trying to include her in your planning, explaining how busy you are, and so forth. She may be one of those difficult mothers-in-law whom you cannot please, no matter how hard you try. What she really wants is your undivided attention, and when you give her that, then she'll just find something else to complain about.

My only other suggestion is to plan a regular weekly dinner with her on a night when you are not so busy. Since you don't have time to cook, use take-out food or grab a quick bite somewhere. Or perhaps you could take your materials and work on a wedding project at her kitchen table while she cooks. If this doesn't satisfy her, then you know that nothing will and that you have given her your best shot.

A bride writes: My fiancé and I have been dating for four years. We had a great relationship with his parents, who are now divorced. Since the engagement, my fiancé's mother has become very distant. When my mother and I attempted to involve her in the wedding plans, she became quite cold. She did say that it was her "duty" to pay for the rehearsal dinner and that she expected no financial help from her ex-husband and his wife (which is not the case). When we suggested the restaurant we preferred, she was very negative. When we tried to explain the sentimental value of the restaurant, she refused to budge, saying that since she was paying for it, she will decide the location. She is the only person in the family who seems to have a problem with this charm-

ing, inexpensive restaurant. Everyone else thinks we should have the opportunity to have the dinner at the location of our choice. —FROZEN OUT

DEAR FROZEN: You are not going to want to hear this, but technically, as hostess, she is supposed to be the one to choose where the dinner will be held. Usually parents want to make their children happy and would select a mutually agreeable site, but this is not the usual situation.

The dinner site is not your real problem. There is something else going on here, that "coldness" and "rudeness" you mentioned. Your fiancé's mother seems to be having difficulty with her emotions as your wedding becomes a reality. This may have to do with her divorce and with her ex-husband's remarriage. Weddings tend to bring the skeletons of a failed marriage out of the closet.

Your fiancé's mother may also be upset with your behavior. It is not a good idea for you and your fiancé to run around and try to get everyone on your side about the restaurant debate. You are backing her into a corner. You would be wise to drop the issue before it blows completely out of proportion.

Invitations and Announcements

Your Presence Is Requested

*I*nvitations set the tone for an event by creating feelings of expectation and excitement in your guests. So why would couples want to cut corners on invitations to the most important event of their lives? Use the best paper you can afford, and don't clutter your lovely formal invitations with stuffers about the other events you've planned or those discount hotel rates you've arranged. Send that material separately.

The traditional invitation to a formal wedding is a large fold-over note accompanied by a smaller reception card. For small ceremonies with large receptions, the invitations will be exactly the reverse. The large invitation is to the reception and the smaller ceremony card that goes to the few guests invited is inserted into the large reception invitations.

And while calligraphy is a nice touch for addresses, it's an unnecessary expense. But please don't use your computer to print out addressed envelopes or—horrors—stick-on labels. Your guests deserve better than that. And so do you. Write out the addresses in your neatest hand.

"How Do We Word the Invitations?"

Traditional formal wedding invitations follow a prescribed format that evolved decades before divorce became so common. Figuring out whose name goes where, especially when there are multiple divorces, can leave couples wondering if they have done the right thing.

If the Bride Has Been Married

A handwritten note or a phone call traditionally has been the means of inviting guests to a small ceremony when the bride was divorced. Handwritten notes are best, but if the wedding will be large, engraved invitations are acceptable. Here are several variations on wording.

• If the bride is a young divorcée, her parents may issue the invitations. These invitations are similar to invitations to a bride's first wedding. The difference is that the bride may have a different last name from her parents if she still uses the name from her first marriage.

∞

Mr. and Mrs. Phillip Hugh Brodowski
request the honour of your presence
at the marriage of their daughter
Frances Marilyn Cartwright
to
Mr. Henry Curtis Lewis, junior

on Saturday, the seventh of April
at four o'clock
Fairview Baptist Church
Denver
and afterward at
Boone Mountain Country Club

• If a woman is a "mature" bride (that's wedding industry lingo for a woman who is older than thirty and no longer lives at home with her parents), she and the groom usually issue the invitations themselves.

Angela Harris Bickel
and
Joseph Hubert Forrester
request the honour of your presence
at their marriage
[or, if you prefer, "invite you to attend their wedding"]
on Saturday, the third of September
at six o'clock
St. Andrew's Presbyterian Church
Yuma, Arizona
and afterward at
Cooper Canyon Country Club

Or

The honour of your presence
is requested
at the marriage of

Angela Harris Bickel
and
Joseph Hubert Forrester
on Saturday, the third of September
Two thousand and two [optional]
at six o'clock
St. Andrew's Presbyterian Church
Yuma, Arizona
and afterward at
Cooper Canyon Country Club

If the Groom Has Been Married

The groom's past will not affect the wording of a wedding invitation. Any of the preceding invitation styles would be appropriate.

If the Bride's Parents Are Divorced

As families divide and multiply these days, a couple can easily find themselves faced with the prospect of an invitation that has more names than a phone book. They want to include the bride's mom and dad, of course, but now they are married to other people. So let's get the current stepmom and stepdad listed, too. That's four. But the bride was closer to her first stepmother than her second. Should she be listed, too?

And then the groom wants his parents' names on the invitations, too. So that's eight because he, too, has dual sets of parents. But what about the aunt and uncle who *really* raised him? Where do their names go?

Whoa! Wedding invitations are not family trees, but how do we word them? In the days when divorce was still considered taboo, figuring out the invitations was easy. It was considered tacky for a divorced couple's names to appear together on a wedding invitation. So the invitations to the ceremony were issued in the name of the bride's mother (and her new spouse, if she had one). As hosts of the reception, the bride's father (and his new spouse) issued those invitations separately. Everything was very civilized and antiseptic.

But having a divorced couples' names on a wedding invitation is no longer considered a sin. Couples (and their spouses) who are amicable frequently share the honors. But if one divorced parent issues the invitation to the ceremony and the other parent hosts the reception, the invitations are mailed separately.

Here are some examples:

Neither Parent Remarried, Invitation Issued Jointly

Mrs. Jones Claiborne
[or Mrs. Margaret Jones Claiborne, whichever she prefers]
Mr. Darrell Christopher Baxter
request the honour of your presence
at the marriage of their daughter
Kelly Michelle
to
Mr. Ronald Bernard LaFrance, junior
on Saturday, the third of September
at six o'clock
St. Martin of the Fields Episcopal Church
Des Moines, Iowa

Please note: A divorced woman usually pairs her maiden name with her married name or her first, maiden, and married names with the title Mrs. or Ms. Please see Names for more information.

Both Parents Remarried, Invitation Issued Jointly

Mr. and Mrs. Robert Wayne Jordan
Mr. and Mrs. Darrell Christopher Baxter
request the honour of your presence
at the marriage of their daughter
Kelly Michelle

to

Mr. Ronald Bernard LaFrance, junior
on Saturday, the third of September
at six o'clock
St. Martin of the Fields Episcopal Church
Des Moines, Iowa

A bride writes: I am a child of divorced parents who have both remarried. I lived with my mom until I went to college, when I moved in with my dad. My parents, who all get along, are sharing the cost of the wedding. I want to give credit where credit is due. How do I word the invitations? —At a Loss for Words

Dear Words: A wedding invitation is not a guide to who has paid for what, with the person who paid the most bills getting the biggest billing. Since your parents and stepparents are friendly, you certainly may put all of your parents' names on the invitation.

A bride writes: My fiancé and I are paying for our wedding ourselves. Out of respect for our parents, we would like to include their names on our wedding invitations. My parents are divorced, and both have remarried. I want to include both of my parents, but I don't think I want to list my stepparents' names. I don't want to hurt any feelings. I also want to word the invitations so that it is evident that my fiancé and I are the hosts. —Names and Rank

DEAR NAMES: You may not want to hurt feelings, but list your parents without your stepparents and you will end up with four very unhappy people.

Invitations should be issued in the name of the hosts. Since you and your fiancé are doing things yourselves, the invitations should look like this:

∞

The honour of your presence
is requested at the marriage of
Miss Flora Vista Dulce
and
Captain Torrence Lincoln McKinley
United States Army
[and so forth]

∞

Your parents' names should be included in any announcements you send to newspapers.

A bride writes: I want to know what to do about my parents. They are divorced, and both have remarried. My father hates my mother's husband. I am afraid to put them in the same room together. I'm not too fond of him, but I kind of want him there, too. What should I put on the invitations? —PARENT TRAPPED

DEAR TRAPPED: Feuding parents should set aside their difficulties for the short time it takes to get a daughter married. You may have to remind them of this, very sweetly, of course. If they cannot avoid being disruptive, perhaps one should volunteer to have urgent business out of town.

If your parents cannot get along, the wedding invitations should be issued by the divorced parent with whom you live or who raised you. A less volatile method of handling the invitations is for you and your fiancé to issue the invitations yourselves.

One Parent Remarried, Invitation Issued Jointly

In this sample invitation, the bride's father has remarried, so his wife's name is included on the invitation.

∞

Mrs. Jones Claiborne
[or Mrs. Margaret Jones Claiborne, if she prefers]
Mr. and Mrs. Darrell Christopher Baxter
request the honour of your presence
at the marriage of their daughter
Kelly Michelle
to
Mr. Ronald Bernard LaFrance, junior
on Saturday, the third of September
at six o'clock
St. Martin of the Fields Episcopal Church
Des Moines, Iowa

∞

Often families prefer to have the invitations issued by the parent (and stepparent) with whom the bride lived as a child. Here are examples.

The Bride's Mother (Not Remarried) Issues the Invitation

In this example, the bride's mother is the only name that appears on the invitation.

∞

Mrs. Jones Claiborne
[or Mrs. Margaret Jones Randall, if she prefers]

requests the honour of your presence
at the marriage of her daughter
Kelly Michelle

to

Mr. Ronald Bernard LaFrance, junior
on Saturday, the third of September
Two thousand and two [optional]
at six o'clock
St. Martin of the Fields Episcopal Church
Des Moines, Iowa

The Bride's Mother and Stepfather Issue the Invitation

If the bride's mother has remarried, then her husband's name appears
as well.

Mr. and Mrs. Robert Wayne Jordan
request the honour of your presence
at the marriage of her daughter
Kelly Michelle Claiborne

to

Mr. Ronald Bernard LaFrance, junior
on Saturday, the third of September
Two thousand and two [optional]
at six o'clock
St. Martin of the Fields Episcopal Church
Des Moines, Iowa

The words "Mrs. Jordan's daughter" or "their daughter" also are
acceptable.

A bride writes: My parents are divorced, and my father will not be contributing much to the wedding. How should the invitations be addressed? "Mrs. Roger Clinton and Mr. Tony Dreher request . . ."? Or should the invitations be in my mother's name alone? Or in my mother's and stepfather's? —NAME GAMES

DEAR GAMES: It once was considered improper for the names of divorced parents to appear together on a daughter's wedding invitations. Today, the rule is that divorced parents' names may appear together on a wedding invitation if their relationship is not in a state of armed warfare. If they get along, go for it. You also may include the name of your mother's new husband.

The Bride's Father (Not Remarried) Issues the Invitation
In this scenario, the bride's father alone is hosting the wedding.

Mr. Darrell Christopher Claiborne
requests the honour of your presence
at the marriage of his daughter
Kelly Michelle

to

Mr. Ronald Bernard LaFrance, junior
on Saturday, the third of September
Two thousand and two [optional]
at six o'clocks
St. Martin of the Fields Episcopal Church
Des Moines, Iowa

The Bride's Father and Stepmother Issue the Invitation
If the bride's father has remarried, then his wife's name appears on the invitation.

Mr. and Mrs. Darrell Christopher Claiborne
request the honour of your presence
at the marriage of his daughter
Kelly Michelle
to
Mr. Ronald Bernard LaFrance, junior
on Saturday, the third of September
Two thousand and two [optional]
at six o'clock
St. Martin of the Fields Episcopal Church
Des Moines, Iowa

The words "Mr. Claiborne's daughter" or "their daughter" also are acceptable.

A bride writes: My parents are divorced and, even though I grew up with my mother, my father will be paying for the wedding. He insists that he and my stepmother be listed first on the invitations. I am afraid it will make my mother feel bad. My stepmother was the reason for the divorce. —Caught in the Middle

Dear Caught: Oh dear, your father is sounding petty. The invitations to the ceremony should be issued in your mother's name, since she was the one who raised you. The invitations to the reception should be issued—in a separate mailing—by your father and his wife because they are hosting it.

A bride writes: My parents are divorced, and my fiancé and I are paying for the wedding, which will be my second. How should the invitations be worded? —Daughter of Divorce

DEAR DAUGHTER: If you are divorced, the most proper thing to do would be to write informal notes to your guests inviting them to the wedding.

If you prefer more formal invitations, you and your fiancé may issue the invitations yourself:

∞

The honour of your presence
is requested at the marriage of
Mrs. Stevens Hubbard
and
Mr. Norman Benton Meeker
[and so forth]

∞

Of course, brides and grooms can make their invitations much more personal by saying she and the groom will "unite with love in holy matrimony" or by inviting guests "to share our joy."

A bride writes: I have ordered my wedding invitations but am now having misgivings about the wording. My parents are divorced, and my father has remarried. I have always lived with my mother, and my relationship with my stepmother is polite, but strained. I am genuinely fond of my future mother-in-law, who is paying for a portion of our wedding. I listed first my mother, then my father, and then my in-laws as the persons giving the wedding and the reception. Was it inappropriate to omit my stepmother's name?
—WORDPLAY

DEAR WORDPLAY: It was inappropriate to omit your stepmother's name because, as your father's wife, she is a hostess of the reception. But what's done is done. It's too late—and too expensive—to worry about your mistake. All you can do is apologize to the lady.

Details, Details!

These details hold true for formal wedding invitations as well as announcements.

• The year is optional on invitations, but it must be used on announcements.

• If the wedding is in a place of worship, then the phrase "the honour of your presence" is used. If the wedding will take place at home, or in a hotel or a garden, then "the pleasure of your company" is used. This has to do with the sanctity of holding a wedding in a sacred place.

• If the city is large and the wedding site is not well known to your guests, then the address goes on the invitation.

• With well-known cities such as New York, San Francisco, and Atlanta, for example, no state is needed. However, a nicely drawn and printed map may be enclosed in the invitations.

• The party after a wedding is called a *reception* if it takes place after one o'clock. It is called a *breakfast* if it occurs earlier.

• The traditional spelling of the words *honour* and *favour* are used on wedding invitations.

• The time for the ceremony typically is written "at four o'clock" or "at half after four o'clock." The abbreviations A.M. and P.M. are too informal and never used, but a couple may substitute "in the morning," "in the afternoon," or "in the evening," if they wish.

• No nicknames, please, and no initials. Names should be written out in full—unless one of you hates your middle name so much that you'll threaten to call off the engagement rather than let it become public knowledge.

• If the word *junior* is used, it is written lowercase, unless it is abbreviated. Then it is capitalized. (I can't explain this one! Go figure!)

A bride writes: Is it proper to have wedding invitations addressed with computer printing? I had planned to do so but have had several negative comments. I have received some invitations addressed by computer and think they look very nice, much nicer than some that were handwritten. —COMPUTER WHIZ

DEAR COMPUTER: Your wedding invitation is probably the most formal invitation you will ever issue for one of the most important occasions of your life. Part of the magic surrounding a wedding is the tradition of doing things properly and with care.

Efficiency and *time saving* are not words associated with a wedding. Otherwise, you would simply put your phone number instead of your address with the RSVP. (And don't get me started about response cards. It's bad enough that people feel they have to use them because guests cannot be bothered to write a correct reply on proper stationery.)

So the answer to your question is *no*, computer labeling is not correct. Although I don't think you need go to the expense of hiring a calligrapher to address your invitations, they do need to be addressed by hand. As for bad handwriting, here's a trick: use a ruler as a guide.

 Tacky, Tacky, Tacky

The latest in tackiness from the wedding industry is the so-called "courtesy invitation." Brides and grooms are being told that they can send invitations to people who live out of town who are not expected to show up for the wedding but who might send a gift anyway. Wrong, wrong, wrong. If there are people who need to be notified of a couple's marriage but whose presence is not wanted at the wedding then they should be sent announcements.

Don't send an invitation unless you truly want the recipient to attend your wedding. Otherwise, you will have situations like the one in which a horrified guest was informed by a bride that he had been sent a "courtesy invitation" and wasn't really expected to show up. If he did come to the wedding, she said, the family would "try to fit him in somewhere." He declined.

Practice writing with a ruler, and you will see how quickly your "bad" handwriting improves.

What About the Groom's Parents?

Until about ten years ago, the groom's parents usually did not have their names on wedding invitations. But that has changed, and couples often wish to include his parents as well as hers. Perhaps the groom's parents may help with paying for the wedding or may feel that their friends and relatives will not recognize his name—a sad but true fact of life in today's complicated, mobile families.

To include the groom's parents, simply add a line under his name.

Mr. and Mrs. Calvin Jefferson Dickerson
request the honour of your presence
at the marriage of their daughter
Jacqueline Jemika
to
Mr. Marcus Antonio Milton
Son of Mr. and Mrs. William Walter Harris
and

 We're Not That Stuffy!

If your wedding will be a more casual than traditional affair, engraved invitations are not for you. Most stationery companies produce a variety of colorful invitations that will fit the tone of your wedding. Often couples choose hues and inks that match their wedding colors.

The wording should be less formal as well, with couples asking guests to join in their celebrations, and so forth. Your wedding stationery store will have examples that can be altered to suit your style.

Mr. and Mrs. Curtis Ray Milton
on Saturday, the fourth of April
at seven o'clock
Beulah Baptist Church
Jacksonville, Florida

Couples need to remember that invitations have only a limited amount of space. Too many lines, and the invitation looks busy. Too many lines, and the printer may have to use a smaller, hard-to-read type.

A mother of the groom writes: My son will be getting married in Sacramento, California. Our family and friends live in San Antonio, Texas, and we would like to host a wedding reception here after the wedding. How should the invitation be worded? Should it be mailed with the wedding invitations or separately? —Texas Mom

Dear Mom: The invitation would not invite guests to a wedding reception but to a party (or reception) "honoring Mr. and Mrs. Slim Jim Pickens." This invitation should be mailed separately.

Reception Cards

The one insert that should be included with the wedding invitation is the reception card, which is often used when the reception takes place in a different location from the ceremony. Reception cards are used when the reception or breakfast location is not given on the wedding invitation. The cards also are a way of freeing up space on the invitation so that all of the parents' names may be listed.

A simple, yet correct way of wording the reception cards is:

∽

Reception
Immediately following the ceremony
Charleston Harbor Yacht Club
1012 Barnett Street

RSVP

∽

RESPONSE CARDS

The phrase, "*Respondez, s'il vous plait,*" or RSVP, means "Respond, if you please" and goes in the lower left-hand corner of the invitation. Other forms of this request are "Please respond" or "Kindly reply." If you wish to include the address on the invitation, you may say, "Kindly respond to 21 Peachtree Memorial Drive, Atlanta, 30309."

There was a time when guests knew to respond with a handwritten note to the address on the back of the invitation envelope. However, responding to invitations is rapidly becoming a lost art. Couples desperate to give their caterers correct head counts have resorted to the convenience of response cards. These engraved cards and envelopes do everything but lick the stamps for manners-challenged guests, but many brides and grooms are continually appalled at how few responses they receive.

When rude guests do not respond, couples have my permission to fight back. Yes, it is tacky to telephone guests to see if they will attend. However, a guest's ignoring the invitation cancels out any sins of tackiness committed by the couple or their mothers.

If you use response cards, do not leave a space for guests to indicate how many people will be attending. Couples who do this risk the chance that guests will assume they can bring the entire neighborhood. Instead, use a simple fill-in-the-blank design:

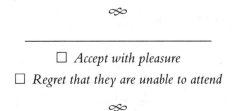

A *bride writes:* My wedding reception will be a black-tie, adults-only affair. Is it tacky to print both "Black Tie Invited" and "Adult Reception" in small print in opposite corners of the invitations? Many of my cousins have small children and they may bring their kids along not knowing what proper etiquette entails. —No Kids Please

Dear No Kids: If your community is a formal community, where men own their own tuxedos, your male guests will know that the dress code for an after-six wedding is black tie. If your community is smaller and less formal, men usually wear dark business suits to six o'clock weddings.

In these rather mannerless times, the smart bride and groom have "Black Tie"—*not* "Invited"—in the lower right-hand corner, but they would *never* say "Adult Reception." That sounds like a movie ratings code.

Most people know not to bring their children if the invitation is not addressed to them. The clever couple handles relatives who might not realize that invitations addressed only to "Mr. and Mrs. Local Yokel" are not meant for their offspring by calling the offending relatives to make sure they understand. In the course of conversation, the clever bride or groom says, "Oh, I wish we could have little Mary and the other children, but this is an adult party—and won't we have fun!" They may enlist their mothers to help with this task.

As a final precaution, the clever bride and groom have a nursery.

FORMAL WEDDING ANNOUNCEMENTS

Couples often have so many friends, relatives, and colleagues, yet not everyone can be invited to the wedding. Sending engraved or printed wedding announcements is a terrific way to share the news.

> A divorced woman who has not remarried usually goes by her maiden name and her married name, for example, Mrs. Jones Stewart. ∞

Similar to wedding invitations, announcements air the couple's good news without inviting anyone to anything. A couple orders announcements when they order the invitations, and the announcements often follow the same style. If the invitation is formal, for example, engraved on fine paper, then the announcements are as well. They are mailed the day of the wedding—*not* when the invitations are mailed.

If the Bride or Groom Has Been Married

The parents of the bride may make the announcement:

Mr. and Mrs. William Wesley Randall
announce the marriage of their daughter
Katherine Randall Hamilton
to
Mr. John Mayes Gibson, junior
on Saturday, the third of September
Two thousand and two
St. Martin of the Fields Episcopal Church
Charleston, South Carolina

Or the couple can do it themselves:

Katherine Randall Hamilton
and
John Mayes Gibson, junior
announce their marriage
on Saturday, the third of September
Two thousand and two
St. Martin of the Fields Episcopal Church
Charleston, South Carolina

If the Parents Are Divorced

If the parents have an amicable relationship, the announcements may
be issued in both names.

Mrs. Jones Randall
[or Mrs. Margaret Jones Randall, depending upon which name she uses]
Mr. William Wesley Randall
announce the marriage of their daughter
Margaret Katherine
to
Mr. John Mayes Gibson, junior
on Saturday, the third of September
Two thousand and two
St. Martin of the Fields Episcopal Church
Charleston, South Carolina

If both parents are remarried, they may issue the announcements
jointly, as in this example.

Mr. and Mrs. Peter Douglas Monroe
Mr. and Mrs. William Wesley Randall
announce the marriage of their daughter
Margaret Katherine Monroe
to
Mr. John Mayes Gibson, junior
on Saturday, the third of September
Two thousand and two
St. Martin of the Fields Episcopal Church
Charleston, South Carolina

In the case of parents who do not get along, the announcements should be issued by the parent who issued the wedding invitations. Please see Names for more information.

Laughter

If We Don't Laugh, We'll Cry

*P*lanning a wedding isn't rocket science. Remember that this whole process is supposed to be fun. When it isn't, you're trying too hard. Back off, take a deep breath, and remember *why* you are doing this. Then worrying about whether guests would prefer beef or chicken falls into perspective.

Above all, keep romance and laughter in your lives. Take a walk together. Make a date for a dinner. Flirt. Read a book that makes you laugh out loud. Watch funny movies. Joke. Giggle. Kid around with your parents. Play games with your kids. Enjoy your life.

Great Wedding Movies
- *Betsy's Wedding*
- *Father of the Bride*—both versions
- *Steel Magnolias*

- *Four Weddings and a Funeral*
- *My Best Friend's Wedding*
- *The Wedding Singer*

"I Want My Wedding to Be Fun This Time"

"I feel like the bride in my mother's wedding," a first-time bride once lamented to me. All too often, parents use their daughter's wedding as a chance to pay back every social invitation they had ever had or to make up for the wedding they wish they'd had. For the bride marrying for the second time, this wedding is a chance to express her personality with an intimate ceremony attended only by the people she cares about, not her parents' friends and acquaintances whom she barely knows.

Let your sense of playfulness and romance prevail. You may decide to have a theme wedding or get married on a mountain or on a beach. One couple rode their horses down the "aisle" made up of their riding pals, all on horseback, too. Another couple had a country wedding with a square dance and barbecue with the bride in white cowgirl boots. Then, there was the couple who threw a black-tie party and—surprise!—just happened to get married in the middle of it.

One Atlanta man proposed to his sweetheart over breakfast, insisting on getting married that day. He had a limo waiting outside to whisk them off for their marriage license, then to Neiman Marcus to buy the bride a dress and have her hair and makeup done. Along the way, they called family and friends via cell phone to invite them to the wedding, held in the garden of a friend, and afterward to dinner in a small, intimate restaurant he had booked for the evening. Their chauffeur even sprang for a bottle of champagne.

Light-hearted invitations will set the tone for your day. One couple from Richmond, Virginia, sent handwritten invitations titled, "Eat,

Drink, and Remarry." A Miami couple's invitations said, "Once Was Not Enough!" And then there was the invitation from a San Francisco couple, Susan "I'll Never Get Married Again!" Chappell and Carl "Do I Look Crazy?" Murray, inviting guests to watch them "eat their words."

Life's short. Have fun.

Music

Here Comes the Bride

We've all heard it so much that it seems as though it isn't a wedding without the familiar strains of Wagner's "Bridal Chorus" from his opera, *Lohengrin*, or of Purcell's "Trumpet Voluntary in D." And brides and grooms usually make their exit to Mendelssohn's "Wedding March" from *A Midsummer Night's Dream*. But there are lots of other selections by Bach, Handel, and other great composers. Be sure to check with your officiant or music director for what it appropriate.

The same goes for a second wedding. Usually the music is scaled down to be in tune with the lower-key ceremony. No thundering strains of traditional marches. No *Lohengrin* or Mendelssohn. No soloists trilling "The Wedding Song." Instead, consider a string quartet or a solo pianist. Again, be sure to check to see what music is acceptable.

Music Notes

• **DON'T** assume you can have any music you choose in a church ceremony. Some churches and synagogues do not permit music for second wedding ceremonies. Others do not permit secular music ever.

• **DO** meet with the officiant or music director to discuss what is available to you. He may even have a tape to give you some examples. This is the time to discuss fees and ask advice about your music selections, musicians, and soloists.

> ∞ "The music at a wedding procession always reminds me of soldiers going into battle."
>
> *—Heinrich Heine*

• **DO** save the popular songs for your wedding reception, not your ceremony.

• **DO** give the deejay or band a list of the songs you want performed at the reception—and the songs you *don't* want performed as well. Not everyone appreciates the raunchy lyrics of today's music.

• **DO** supply the deejay with a recording of your special song for your first dance. Give it to him at the reception. If you have a band, make sure they can play it to your satisfaction.

• **DO** negotiate beforehand about breaks for the band or deejay. You can pay them to play straight through.

WEDDING ANNOUNCERS

Band leaders or deejays often act as emcees for wedding receptions by introducing the couple and their wedding party, announcing that the couple will cut the cake, making corny jokes, and so forth. If you don't want to risk having your reception being ruined by a cheesy version of Ed McMahon, tell the guy to cool it. It's your wedding. If you don't want introductions or announcements, even though they may be customary in your part of the country, you need not have them. The band's job, after all, is to play music.

Save the First Dance for Me

When the music begins, the bride and groom usually take to the dance floor alone to a favorite song. Many couples who love to dance find that showing off their fancy footwork is a sure crowd pleaser, but those with two left feet may simply make an obligatory turn around the room.

Then the bride's father traditionally breaks in to dance with his daughter, so the groom then dances with his mother. Then the groom dances briefly with the bride's mother while the bride is whirled about by her new father-in-law.

The bride's father then dances with the groom's mother and the groom's father with the bride's mother as the bridesmaids and groomsmen join them. The bride and groom dance with guests.

Couples often make themselves crazy trying to adapt this beloved tradition to today's blended families. If tensions are high, the couple may invite all of the guests to dance after they have their traditional dance, thus foregoing the dance with the parents.

A Sour Note?

First it was conga lines. Then the hokeypokey. The latest in reception fun is dance contests celebrating the "longest marriage." Couples bow out as their anniversary is called—one week, a year, ten years, and so forth, until the longest married couple is the only one left on the dance floor. Warn the announcer to skip this if the parents of the bride and groom are on their second or third marriages.

A bride who wants to honor her stepfather may choose to have the father-daughter dance with him if her natural father escorted her during the ceremony.

After the groom dances with his mother-in-law, he then dances with his mother and with his stepmother, if he chooses.

Everyone involved should be informed ahead of time as to the order of the dance, especially if the couple makes any changes in the traditional order.

Names

The Name Game

"The Name Game" can be another obstacle on the way to wedded bliss for couples. Although the bride is free to select whichever option she is most comfortable with, she needs to consider her children's names, her professional reputation and—perhaps most importantly—her fiancé's feelings.

After the Wedding

A woman who has never been married before has the option of:

- Taking her new husband's name
- Keeping her maiden name

A woman who has been married before has the option of:

- Keeping her surname from a previous marriage
- Taking her new husband's name
- Returning to or keeping her maiden name

A bride writes: I cannot believe how judgmental some of my unmarried friends are when they hear that I plan to take my husband's name after our marriage. We plan to have children and think this would be best for us as a family. It hurts my feelings that they are so unsupportive. What should I say to them? —Proud to Be Mrs.

Dear Proud: "Frankly, my dears, I don't give a damn." Well, maybe not those exact words, but that is your attitude. When one of these so-called "friends" makes a catty remark, stare at her for a brief minute, then say, "Oh, really?" in a bemused voice before turning your attention and the subject to something else. They'll get the message that their unsolicited opinions are not welcome.

After the Divorce

A woman does not keep her husband's name after a divorce because she is no longer Mrs. James Warren Wilson. Instead, if she wants to keep the Mrs., she pairs her maiden name with her married name: Mrs. Smith Wilson. Or she can become Ms. Marie Smith Wilson with her maiden name as a middle name.

A woman who marries for a second time drops her married surname (from her first husband) and adds her new married name: Mrs. Marie Smith Jones.

Of course, women can avoid all of this by keeping their maiden names when they marry or by reverting to their maiden names when they divorce.

*A bride writes: My fiancé feels very strongly that I should take his name once we are married, but I would prefer keeping my maiden name for professional reasons. The latest wedding planner I received states, "If you are taking your husband's name, change your driver's license, and so forth" as if it were a common option not to change one's name. What is the current etiquette on this topic? How can I convince my fiancé that my name is as important to me as his name is to him? —*BEWILDERED BRIDE

DEAR BEWILDERED: Although I have seen no statistics on it, most women I see still continue the tradition of changing their names, especially if they are younger and have not yet made a name for themselves professionally or if they plan to have children.

Many women keep their maiden names for professional and legal reasons, yet go by their married names on social occasions. Some couples even combine their last names, and both the man and the woman change. The nice thing is that today we have these options, and, while it may be difficult for some people to accept, it is no longer such a stigma to keep our maiden names.

Dealing with your fiancé is another matter. You may offer to compromise and use your maiden name professionally and your married name socially, but this is something only the two of you can decide.

Try role-playing with your fiancé. Ask him to put himself in your place. Would he want to be called by *your* last name? You could even go so far as to send him mail addressed that way. That way, perhaps he can understand your reservations.

*A bride writes: This will be my second marriage. I have been divorced for four years, but I still go by my married name, mainly for the sake of my seven-year-old son. Could I put my maiden name on the wedding invitation? I have already been introduced to my future family by my married name. —*NAME GAME

DEAR GAME: One cannot simply change one's name on a whim. After your divorce, you did not go through the legal steps to return to your maiden name. Your wedding invitations should carry your current legal name.

A bride writes: This is my second marriage, and my two children and I will assume my husband's name. Is it appropriate to include the children's names on the "at-home" cards as a way of letting people know what names they'll be using? If not, what is the proper way? —A BRIDE AND A MOM

DEAR BRIDE-MOM: Your "at-home" cards are for you and your husband. Write notes to close friends and family to pass along the good news about your youngsters' new last names.

A bride writes: I am marrying for the second time. My fiancé and I will issue our invitations, but I don't know what names to use. Legally, I retained my married name because of my son, but I am using my maiden name on a regular basis. The name I use professionally is Debbie P. (Crockett) Garland. Would that be appropriate for the invitations as well? My fiancé goes by his nickname, not his given name. Should the invitations read Nelson W. "Dusty" Rhodes (his given name and his nickname) or just his nickname, Dusty W. Rhodes? —CONFUSED

DEAR CONFUSED: Formal engraved invitations should include the full legal names of the bride and groom—no initials, no parentheses, and no nicknames. Your name would appear as Deborah Crockett Garland and your fiancé's as Nelson William Rhodes. However, if your wedding is small and informal, which is usually the case for a second-time bride, you certainly may use nicknames. But, parentheses do not belong on an invitation.

Newspaper Announcements

Have You Heard the News Today?

*A*fter your families have been informed of your engagement, it's time to tell the world. Becoming engaged to be married is a momentous step in the rituals of our lives, and it deserves special recognition. And it goes without saying that your wedding itself is a newsworthy event. Many couples publish announcements of their engagements and weddings in their hometown newspapers. Often their photographs are used as well. Most newspapers publish engagement and wedding announcements without charge. Usually the features department of your local paper has a clerk who will send you fill-in-the-blank forms. With that information, a newspaper employee will write the story. Some small-town papers will publish your photo and story just as you write it without charge. Still other publications, usually in large cities, will charge you by the inch for a story and a photo.

In that case, you are responsible for writing the story, and the longer it is, the more it costs.

Be sure to include the name and phone number of a contact when you submit your story and make sure that your name and number are on your photo. The editor needs to be able to find you if she has questions about your story. This also helps ensure that your photo is published with your name and not someone else's!

The way the story is written reveals that the bride's or groom's parents have been divorced (and remarried) without stating the obvious. Stepparents should be included in the write-up. This example shows that the bride's mother and the groom's father have remarried.

> Mr. and Mrs. Robert Wayne Miller of Atlanta and Mr. Albert Byron East of Tampa announce the engagement of their daughter, Karen Melinda East, to Mr. Joseph Christopher Stephens, son of Mrs. Diana Davis Stephens and Mr. and Mrs. James Gregory Stephens, all of Birmingham.

Information for Newspaper Story About the Engagement
- Full name of the bride-to-be
- Full name of the future groom
- Month and place that the ceremony will be held
- Names of both sets of parents, including stepparents
- Names of deceased parents, for example, "the late Mr. Rodney Maxwell Poole"
- Names of grandparents, alive or deceased, if they are known in the town where the story appears
- Cities where everyone resides (Don't include your street address for safety reasons.)
- Careers of the couple
- Any newsworthy fact about the couple, families, or wedding, such as prominent relatives or outstanding accomplishments
- Date of publication

Here is an example of an engagement announcement when the bride's parents are divorced and the groom's parents are remarried and living in different cities.

> Mrs. Angela Dean Shivers and Mr. Richard A. Shivers of Atlantic City announce the engagement of their daughter, Tina Marie Shivers, to Mr. Timothy B. Umbarger of New York City. He is the son of Mr. and Mrs. Garrett V. Walden of Montclair and Mr. and Mrs. Daniel H. Umbarger of Trenton. Miss Shivers is a graduate of Converse College, Spartanburg, South Carolina, and is a reporter for WNJT in Trenton. A graduate of Purdue University, Mr. Umbarger is a political consultant who served as President George W. Bush's campaign advisor. His late grandfather, Mr. Daniel T. Umbarger, served two terms as Secretary of State in New Jersey. The wedding will take place June 8 at the First Presbyterian Church in Trenton. [Or you may say, "A June wedding is planned."]

Information for Newspaper Story About the Wedding
Same as above, plus:

- Names of their children, if the couple has been married before
- Couple's educational background
- Clubs, fraternities, or professional organizations
- Military service
- Names and cities of residence of members of wedding party (optional)
- Place and style of the reception
- Wedding trip
- Location of new residence (Again, omit your street address.)
- Optional descriptions of wedding party's attire (This occurs more frequently in small-town newspapers.)

In this sample wedding announcement, the bride's parents are remarried and the groom's father is deceased.

Vanessa Leurise Matthews and Alejandro Andre Charles Jr. were married at 2 o'clock on May 9 at Southwest Christian Church in Lincoln, Nebraska. The Rev. Wallace Avery officiated. A reception immediately followed at the Raiford Inn. The bride is the daughter of Mr. and Mrs. Clarence Collins Denny of Lincoln and Mr. and Mrs. Gary Craig Matthews of Columbus. The groom is the son of Mrs. Alejandro A. Charles of Omaha and the late Mr. Charles. [If you wish, you can include your grandparents' names and residences here.]

The bride is a magna cum laude graduate of the University of Nebraska and is employed as an occupational therapist at the Nebraska Division of Rehabilitation Services.

The groom, who also graduated from the University of Nebraska, is employed as a risk manager with Goodson Insurance Co. while pursuing a graduate degree in business. He is a veteran of the U.S. Navy. [The next paragraphs should contain the names of the wedding party. In some parts of the country, it is also customary to describe the bride's attire and/or any parties given for the couple.]

The couple honeymooned in Jamaica. They will live in Omaha.

IF THE BRIDE OR GROOM HAS BEEN MARRIED

Some newspapers report that a bride or groom was previously married in their wedding write-ups, but most do not mention it. It is up to you if you wish to include a line saying "The bride was married previously" or "The bride was widowed" in an engagement or wedding announcement.

Wedding announcements usually include the names of children, such as "Mrs. Moore has three children from a previous marriage,

Anna Elizabeth, Mary Louise, and Polly Margaret Adams." Or "Mrs. Moore's three daughters, Anna Elizabeth, Mary Louise, and Polly Margaret Adams, participated in the afternoon ceremony."

Here is an example of a wedding announcement when the bride and groom have been married before.

> Margaret Lindsey Owens and Paul Stephen Butler were married May 9 in Bethlehem Methodist Church in Martins Ferry. The Rev. John M. Jennings officiated. The bride and groom were attended by their children. A reception immediately followed the ceremony.
>
> The bride, the daughter of Mrs. Michael T. Lindsey of Martins Ferry and the late Mr. Lindsey, is an attorney with Matthews, Hutchins, and Ade in Toledo. A graduate of Miami of Ohio University, she is president of the Toledo chapter of the American Association of University Women and a member of the board of the Toledo Women's Foundation. She has three children, Jennifer, Cindy, and Adam, from a previous marriage.

 Dead Wrong

Don't make this mistake. A deceased parent cannot announce the engagement or wedding of a son or daughter. Instead, find a spot to insert the phrase, "daughter of the late Mr. Rodney Maxwell Poole." The same goes if the groom has a deceased parent.

For example: Mr. and Mrs. Mark Whitlock McKee announce the engagement of their daughter, Julie Dianne, to James Gregory Stephens Jr., son of Mr. James Gregory Stephens of St. Paul and the late Mrs. Stephens."

The groom, who holds a Ph.D. from Miami of Ohio University, is a professor of history at the University of Toledo and has authored several books on World War II, including *Germany at War*. The son of Mr. and Mrs. William A. Butler of Steubenville, he has one son from a previous marriage, Paul Stephen Butler Jr.

After a wedding trip to New York, the couple will live in Toledo.

Photography and Videography

Just One Big Happy Family

O ne of the emotional minefields that couples must negotiate during a wedding is how to capture their families on film when their families are no longer intact. The bride or groom who tries to reunite his or her family just for the sake of the wedding photos is doomed to disappointment when divorced parents who hate each other's guts refuse to go along with the plan.

A little advance preparation may soothe tensions and alleviate hurt feelings. Tell your divorced parents that you would like photos of them and their new spouses with you both, but you would also like a photo with your mom and dad—without the stepparent. This advance approach may work better than springing your request on everyone at the reception. The gracious stepparent will willingly step aside. If he or she will not cooperate, at least you will know ahead of time and spare yourself an awkward scene on your wedding day.

Photography and Videography Tips

• Always hire a professional. Don't depend on a friend to do this job for you, or you may end up with photos and videotape only of people the amateur shooter knows. You only have one chance to "do it right," so don't take any chances.

• Decide beforehand what kinds of shots you want before the reception and limit the photographer's time in getting them. You don't want to arrive at the reception an hour late. Make sure the photographer and videographer have a list of scenes, such as cutting the cake or tossing the bouquet.

• Specify where the videographer and his assistant will be during the ceremony. Unless you state that they should film from the balcony or some other unobtrusive spot, you may find them shooting from the altar or under the chuppah.

• Price your photographer's package of traditional shots (for example, of the wedding party, of each family) instead of ordering them à la carte, which can be more expensive. If there is something special you want, perhaps the two of you with your ring bearer, then ask if that can be swapped out for something you don't want.

• Give a few trusted guests disposable cameras to snap candid moments at the reception. Many couples have found that having too many disposable cameras is a distraction. Everyone is so busy snapping photos, no one enjoys the party!

All Together Now . . . Say Rice!

Some couples get around the sticky questions of who poses with whom by including the entire extended family in a photograph.

• Watch out for extra costs, such as overpriced frames or albums or extra copies of the video.

• If your contract calls for photographs or videotapes to be delivered to you by a certain date, make sure the contract includes a penalty for not meeting the deadline.

A bride writes: My parents are divorced and have been remarried to others for some time. How am I to take the pictures without hurting my stepparents' feelings? —Extra Parents

Dear Extra: When it's time for pictures, have the photographer shoot several poses of you and the groom with various family groupings. This can be arranged with the photographer and your parents ahead of time so you can make sure everyone—stepparents, too—is included in at least one pose.

You may ask your parents if they will pose with you and your new husband or wife without their spouses, but unless they get along well, they may decline.

Premarital
Counseling

"Let's Get It Right This Time"

*T*oo often, I receive letters from brides who sound as though they have given more thought to what color nail polish their bridesmaids will wear than to what the institution of marriage really means. Of course, we all know that marriage is more than selecting china that he and she both like or sharing a checking account. When it comes to planning a wedding, we know how to make sure our guests have a glorious time, but do we really know how to put on a marriage?

If you are reading this book, there is an almost 100 percent chance that you or someone you love has gone through a divorce. I don't need to tell you what a horrible experience that was for everyone, especially for children. Each year more than one million kids watch their parents' marriages end. And the divorce rate for second marriages—more than 60 percent—proves that "starter marriages" are not good practice for marrying again.

It's a good idea for couples to have premarital counseling whether this is their first marriage or an encore performance. Visiting a counselor or clergy person or taking a course is a way to develop realistic expectations of marriage and avoid repeating past mistakes or copying our parents'. After all, we take lessons in learning to drive a car. Why not instructions before we begin the most important journey of our lives?

What is premarital counseling? It's more than a quiz to determine if two people truly love one another or if they're compatible. It helps them explore the issues that arise in marriage: money, in-laws, sex, communication, religion and morals, children, discipline, anger, disappointment. Studies show that couples who take premarital counseling courses build a firmer foundation for marriages that last.

> ∞ "Marriage is our last, best chance to grow up."
>
> —Joseph Barth

One concern people have is that premarital counseling will end their relationship. "What if I find out she's not the right one?" "What if we discover that we don't agree on anything important?" Better now than after you have spent tens of thousands of dollars on a wedding or, worse yet, had children together. Divorce is an expensive way to fix a mistake.

Fortunately, there are people who see how important the institution of marriage is to our society and the well-being of our children. These people are teachers and scholars, marriage counselors and therapists, psychologists and social workers, religious and government leaders, policy analysts, divorce lawyers, and legal reformers, even governors. They are determined to strengthen marriage and have championed laws that make it more difficult to divorce, require mediation in divorce cases, lift the marriage tax penalty, provide marriage classes for high school kids, and propose other remedies. They also advocate courses to develop skills in handling conflict and expressing love, intimacy, and appreciation within marriage.

Today, more than a third of people under age forty are children of divorce. According to therapist Judith Wallerstein's *The Unexpected Legacy of Divorce*, the most serious effects of divorce arise in early adulthood when children of divorce begin to have serious relationships. They live in intense fear that the happiness of a relationship will be snatched from them. This is not a legacy we should be proud of.

> "What counts in making a happy marriage is not so much how compatible you are, but how you deal with incompatibility."
> —*Leo Tolstoy*

Most religions now require that the engaged couple meet with their clergy person before they can be married in church. Others require couples to go through counseling courses that are more detailed. In either case, couples should be prepared to discuss any past divorces and the reasons for them. It's also a good idea to think about why other marriages in the family have failed and what lessons can be learned.

With the divorce rate so high and so many children being raised in single-parent homes, many states are considering requiring couples to take premarital counseling before they can get marriage licenses. Florida has enacted a "look before you leap" law giving couples who take four hours of counseling a big discount on their marriage license fee. Florida high schools also now offer marriage courses.

This kind of course is available to couples planning to marry as well as those whose marriages are in trouble or who want to strengthen their marriages. For more information, ask your clergy person or local United Way organization. Information also is available on the Web at www.smartmarriages.com or www.marriagemovement.org.

I discovered these resources too late for my marriage, but I plan to learn skills for a happy marriage before I try it again. I hope you also will consider a course in marriage as important to your wedding preparations as selecting your wedding rings. My goal is to make this book obsolete.

∞ "The divorce laws have it all wrong. 'Irreconcilable differences'—like a bad knee or a chronic backache—are part of all good marriages. Successful couples learn to dance in spite of their differences."
—Diane Sollee, marriage counselor

A bride writes: We're engaged and have set a date, but I am afraid. Divorce seems to run in my family. Not only are my parents divorced, but also my grandparents. My fiancé's parents also are divorced, and we both have aunts, uncles, and cousins who have divorced. While I think divorce should be an option for some marriages, this seems excessive. Is divorce genetically programmed in my family? I have seen how much pain it causes. What can I do to give my marriage a better chance? —ANXIOUS BRIDE

DEAR ANXIOUS: Although your family may appear to be doomed to divorce, there is no divorce jinx haunting your relatives. With a divorce rate of 50 percent, divorce has become as much a part of our lives as marriage. And a recent study shows that children whose parents are divorced are 76 percent more likely to divorce themselves.

Make planning for your marriage together even more important than planning for your wedding. Courses in marriage skills can help the two of you learn how to handle the inevitable conflict in your marriage and keep your romance alive. Ask your clergy person for help in finding a course right for you or research courses via websites such as www.smartmarriages.com.

Prenuptial
Agreements

"Sure I Love You, But . . ."

*D*on't have a million? Don't worry. Prenuptial agreements are no longer limited to those in financial stratospheres. Marla Trump may have had the most publicized prenup recently, but agreements in case of divorce—no matter how farfetched the possibility—are increasing, especially for couples with considerable assets and/or children.

Usually, women are the ones asked to sign prenups because men usually have more assets to protect, but the agreements can be mutual. Prenuptial agreements can avoid messy courtroom battles over money in the case of divorce while protecting one's financial assets for one's children or oneself.

What is a prenuptial agreement? A prenup, as it is commonly called, is a contract between two people that spells out how assets will be divided in case of divorce or death. Such agreements have existed since Biblical times, when rich families wanted to protect their wealth. They became popular in the nineteenth century to protect young heiresses from men who wanted to marry them for their money.

If I could change anything about my wedding, I would pay closer attention to our prenuptial agreement. I wanted to be fair to my husband's children from a former marriage, but I ended up shortchanging myself. ∞

Should a bride or groom feel insulted if asked to sign a prenuptial agreement? A marriage is a peculiar blend of religious and civil contracts, and a man or woman who has been burned by divorce and alimony payments may feel a need to be protected from a repeat performance.

A marriage also is a unique bond of trust between two people. Counselors often argue that a prenuptial agreement starts a marriage badly by assuming there will be a divorce. The prenuptial destroys that trust, they say. But a prenuptial agreement also can give each partner and their children a sense of financial security. Each couple will have to decide for themselves whether a prenup should be part of their wedding plans.

Who should have prenuptial agreements? According to Joseph P. Zwack, an attorney and author of *Premarital Agreements: When, Why and How to Write Them*, people should consider having one if they:

- Own assets such as a home, stocks, or a business
- Have children or grandchildren from a previous marriage
- Are much wealthier than the other partner
- Have loved ones, such as elderly parents, who will need care

What steps should a bride or groom take when asked to sign a prenuptial? The couple should have his and her lawyers. Both partners should contribute to the contract, and they must reveal all of their assets. Ideally, the document should be signed at least a month before the wedding so that it will not appear that the document was signed under duress. One financial planner advises the couple to sign before the wedding invitations are mailed.

As in all legal contracts, read it carefully before you sign it. And if you feel uncomfortable about it, get a second opinion from another attorney. If you still feel uncomfortable, don't sign it.

During the marriage, the agreement should be reviewed periodically and updated as the couple's finances change, if children arrive, and so forth.

> ∞ "Being divorced is like being hit by a Mack truck. If you live through it, you start looking very carefully to the right and to the left."
>
> —*Jean Kerr, author*

Is there anything couples can do to show they still trust each other? Prenups may be signed after the wedding. To avoid that "Honey, I trust you, but . . ." syndrome, couples can agree to sign the document after they say "I do." This way, both are acting on good faith. And some couples design their prenuptial agreements to expire after a certain time limit.

Are prenuptial agreements written in stone? Not necessarily. Prenups can be set aside in cases of fraud, duress, unfairness, failure to disclose, and failure to be adequately represented.

Receiving Lines

The Lineup

*R*eceiving lines are always held for formal weddings and breakfasts, either at the reception site or at the site of the ceremony just after the wedding. Receiving lines are optional at semiformal receptions and rarely held at an informal wedding.

Occasionally, a bride and groom do not want to "waste time" standing in line, or perhaps they do not want the formality of a line, but receiving lines really are the most efficient way for the couple and their families to greet and thank every guest. If a couple decides not to receive, they may greet guests by going from table to table during the meal.

Here's the traditional makeup of a receiving line:

- The bride's mother
- The groom's father (optional)

- The groom's mother
- The bride's father (optional)
- The bride
- The groom
- The maid or matron of honor
- The bridesmaids, in the same order as the processional (optional)

If the officiant stands in the line (a rare occurrence), he or she stands between the bride and her father.

Fathers are not required in receiving lines, although they are a nice decorative touch. If the bride's father does not want to participate, then the groom's father stands next to the bride.

When a parent is deceased. If the bride's father is dead, the bride's mother may receive alone. If she has remarried, her husband may or may not receive with her, whatever the bride prefers.

If the bride's mother is dead, her father takes the mother's position in the receiving line or he may ask a female relative to receive with him. If he has remarried, his wife receives with him.

Although the bride's parents are usually hosts of the reception, the above rules also apply to the groom's parents if they act as hosts.

Divorced parents. This is where it gets tricky. It helps to remember that whoever is giving the wedding reception should be considered the host or the hostess. Strictly speaking, both divorced parents should not stand in the line, just as traditionally their names did not appear together on their child's wedding invitation. Thus, if the father is giving the reception, his new spouse is considered the hostess and stands in the receiving line. The bride's mother is considered an honored guest and does not stand in the line.

However, as divorce has become more commonplace—and more amicable, in many cases—this rule has relaxed. If both parents are hosting the reception, they may both appear in the line. If the bride is close to her stepmother, the stepmother may choose to stand in the line as hostess as well. Usually the bride's stepfather does not stand in the line.

However, if divorced parents do not get along, the simplest ways may be best. Omit the men from the receiving line, which then consists only of the bride and groom and their mothers. The couple also may receive alone, if they chose.

Here is the lineup when the bride's parents are divorced:

- The bride's mother
- The groom's father (optional)
- The groom's mother
- The bride
- The groom
- The bride's stepmother (optional)
- The bride's father (optional; if he is in line, his current wife should be as well)
- The maid or matron of honor
- The bridesmaids, in the same order as the processional (optional)

If the bride's father and his new wife are hosting the reception, then the bride's mother is attending as an honored guest and does not stand in the receiving line:

- The bride's father
- The bride's stepmother
- The groom's father (optional)
- The groom's mother
- The bride
- The groom
- The maid or matron of honor
- The bridesmaids, in the same order as the processional (optional)

A bride writes: My parents are divorced, and my mother raised me alone. My father never showed much interest in me as a child, so my mother will escort me down the aisle. What about a receiving line at the reception? —DOING WITHOUT DAD

DEAR DOING WITHOUT: You, your new husband, and both of your mothers (and grandmothers, if you choose) would form the receiving line at the reception.

A mother of the groom writes: Who stands in the receiving line at the reception? Joey's father and I divorced when he was four, and we both have remarried. Joey grew up with me, seeing his father only once a year. Joey wants me and my husband and his father—but not his stepmother—to stand in the line. I have never heard of this and frankly am very uncomfortable with this situation. My ex-husband and I are civil and polite, but far from friendly. I feel that my husband and I should stand in the receiving line since we are the ones who raised him. —Groom Gloom

DEAR GLOOM: Technically your ex-husband and his new wife are attending the wedding as guests and should not be part of the receiving line. However, if everyone can put aside their disagreements for the thirty to forty-five minutes you will be in line, it would be a nice gesture to include your ex-husband and his wife. What would not be correct is Joey's idea, because it is an insult to his stepmother to omit her. His dad and his new wife are considered a unit socially.

 ## Receiving Line Rules to Live By

Rule number one: Divorced parents do not stand next to one another unless they get along extremely well.

Rule number two: If a divorced father stands in line, his new wife should be at his side.

Here is the lineup when the groom's parents are divorced:

- The bride's mother
- The groom's father (optional)
- The groom's stepmother (optional; if he's in line, she should be, too)
- The bride's father (optional)
- The bride
- The groom
- The groom's mother
- The groom's stepfather (optional)
- The maid or matron of honor
- The bridesmaids, in the same order as the processional (optional)

It is not necessary to have any of the fathers in the receiving line at all. This would get you off the hook. Talk to the bride's mother. It is perfectly permissible to have just the bride's father and omit the groom's father and stepfather.

"WHERE DO WE RECEIVE OUR GUESTS?"

Many couples choose to receive their guests as they enter the reception hall, but the couple also may choose to stand in another part of the room so that guests do not have to stand in line to get in the door. A couple also has the option of receiving guests as they exit the wedding site immediately after the ceremony. Couples who invite more people to the ceremony than to the reception should receive at the wedding site.

If the reception is a seated dinner, the bride and groom may go from table to table greeting their guests. The drawback is that often they do not know exactly who's who. With a receiving line, each guest is introduced by name.

RECEIVING LINE TIPS

The receiving line should be organized so that the bride is greeted before the groom because traditionally her mother and father, as hostess and host, are first in line. If a formal wedding is huge (we're talking a cast of thousands), the bride's mother cannot be expected to know every guest's name. This is where an announcer, who stands first in line, comes in handy. Guests give their names to him, and he then repeats the name to the bride's mother.

Each person in the line greets a guest and passes the guest along to the person to the left with a bit of explanation: "Mrs. Hill, I'd like you to meet my husband, John. John darling, this is Mrs. Hill, who was my first-grade teacher."

Those in the receiving line should keep it short and sweet—a greeting and a thank you—to avoid holding up the line: "Thank you for coming." "We are so glad you could be with us." "Mrs. Hill, Sarah has told me so much about you. Thank you for coming. I'd like you to meet my stepmother, Anne Phillips."

Guests also should keep it short and sweet: "Maria, you look lovely. You and Alonzo have our best wishes." Or "Mrs. Garcia, the wedding was beautiful. I've never seen a more handsome couple. They look so happy together."

At a formal wedding, the women in the line wear their gloves while the men remove theirs.

Snacking is a no-no. We don't want to greet guests with our mouths full. However, it is permissible to sneak a sip of champagne.

Receptions

It's Party Time!

$\mathcal{W}$eddings are a unique blend of religious, civil, and social ceremonies. While religious practices usually dictate the style of the ceremony, the reception can be a true reflection of a couple's personality.

TYPES OF RECEPTIONS

These range from less expensive to flat-out bank-busting.

Morning

A wedding breakfast or brunch, ideal for small and second weddings, is usually held at a restaurant or club, but can be held at the couple's home. A classical musician is a nice touch.

Afternoon

The afternoon party is often a stand-up affair at a church, club, or home. Food may be simple (punch and finger sandwiches) or a more elaborate buffet with alcoholic drinks, tea, and coffee. Music can be classical, or if you want dancing, have rock 'n' roll or swing supplied by a deejay.

Evening

The evening reception ranges from a fancy cocktail buffet all the way to a sit-down dinner with a cocktail hour beforehand. Music for dancing is supplied by a deejay or a band. A reception this elaborate usually follows a formal wedding.

EAT, DRINK, AND BE MERRY

The reception usually lasts from two to four hours and, like any good story, has a beginning, a middle, and an end. You may alter this general schedule to fit your needs. As you plan, remember that shooting your wedding pictures can take as long as thirty to sixty minutes, unless they are shot before the wedding.

Buffet Style

During the first half hour, the following activities take place:

- Guests arrive and are received by the bride, the groom, and their mothers. If the wedding party is delayed due to taking photographs, guests are served drinks and hors d'oeuvres, and the receiving line is formed after the couple arrives.
- Guests sign the bride's book.

- Cocktails and hors d'oeuvres are served.
- Background music plays.

A half hour into the reception:

- The buffet may already be set up when guests arrive, or the food may be placed on the buffet about thirty minutes after the first guests arrive.
- Dancing begins. The bride and groom have the first dance, then dance with their parents. The wedding party joins in and then the guests. (Please see Music for details.)
- Toasts are offered to the couple.
- The couple cuts the cake and eats the first slice. Guests are served cake.
- More dancing!

During the last half hour:

- The bride throws her bouquet. The groom removes the garter (optional).
- The couple slips away to change into their going-away clothes (optional).
- The couple leaves in a rain of rose petals.
- The bar closes and music stops.

Seated Dinner

During the first hour:

- Guests arrive and are received by the bride, the groom, and their mothers. If the wedding party is delayed due to taking photographs, guests are served drinks and hors d'oeuvres, and the receiving line is formed after the couple arrives.
- Guests sign the bride's book.
- Cocktails and hors d'oeuvres are served.
- Background music plays.

During the second hour:

- When the last guest is received, the bride and groom lead the way into the dining room, where dinner is served.
- Toasts are offered to the couple.
- Dancing may begin after the first course or after the entrée is served. The bride and groom have the first dance, then dance with their parents, who next dance with each other. The wedding party joins in and then the guests. (Please see Music for details.)
- The rest of the dinner is served. The couple may opt either to have the band play softly throughout dinner or to play music between courses so guests may dance.
- The couple cuts the cake and eats the first slice. Guests are served cake.
- More dancing!

During the last hour:

- The bride throws her bouquet. The groom removes the garter (optional).
- The couple slips away to change into their going-away clothes (optional).
- The couple leaves in a rain of rose petals.
- The bar closes and music stops.

Tacky, Tacky, Tacky

Some couples are borrowing a lovely trend from Hispanic weddings, where the bride and groom are seated at a romantic table for two. What is not so charming is the trend to serve the bride and groom a different meal. Guests at one wedding noticed when they were served chicken while the bride and groom feasted on lobster.

AT-HOME RECEPTIONS

Receptions at home are fairly inexpensive—unless you get carried away and tent your backyard or redecorate your house. Keep your guest list to fewer than twenty-five people. Remember the budget-busting reception in Steve Martin's *Father of the Bride*.

If you want to save money, don't schedule your wedding for a Saturday night. Saturdays are peak demand time when wedding vendors are busiest and can charge more for their services. Pick an off-peak time—such as Friday night or Sunday—and you may find that you can get more for your money.

THE MASTER OF CEREMONIES

Formal weddings and weddings in some parts of the country often have a master of ceremonies (or a member of the band) who introduces the couple, the wedding party, and the families.

Couples often complain of attending weddings where a lounge lizard emcee takes over and turns what was a lovely party into a raucous bash. This can be especially embarrassing when a smarmy emcee attempts to introduce divorced and remarried families. These tacky public "introductions" need not be done, particularly if a receiving line is held. Limit any announcements to the introduction of the couple.

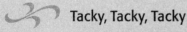 **Tacky, Tacky, Tacky**

Some couples ask about having a cash bar at their wedding reception. When someone comes to your house, sits in your living room, and you serve them wine, do you say, "That'll be will be five dollars please?" Or do you do the polite thing and let them run a tab?

Putting Friends to Work

Not everyone can be a bridesmaid or groomsman, so couples often ask friends and relatives to help out at the reception. This is considered an honor. But the considerate couple makes sure their helpers are not stuck "on the job" during the entire reception. They give everyone a schedule so everyone has time for fun.

Here are some of the tasks that may be assigned to friends:

- Inviting guests to sign the bride's book
- Pouring punch, coffee, or tea (at small informal weddings)
- Passing out wedding cake (at informal weddings), but leave the cutting to the pros
- Greeting guests at the entrance
- Supervising the buffet or passing finger foods (at small informal weddings)
- Making sure the groom's parents are enjoying themselves (if they are from out of town)
- Circulating among the guests and making sure they are enjoying themselves, especially any elderly or out-of-town guests
- Passing out rose petals, birdseed, bubbles, or whatever will be tossed at the departing couple
- Passing out favors, if used, to guests

If I could change anything about my wedding, I would not have the entire wedding party introduced at the reception. Dave and I had to wait around on the bridesmaids and the groomsmen who were drinking and talking and not paying attention to the schedule. It was our wedding. We should not have had to wait.

∞

A mother of the bride writes: At our sit-down reception, we are offering a choice of beef, poultry, or a vegetarian plate. The caterer needs a head count prior to the wedding. May we request this information on the response cards? We thought we would put "Entrée Request" and then list the choices. I am not sure if this is correct. —A GOOD HOSTESS

DEAR HOSTESS: When someone comes to your home for a dinner party, do you ask them in advance what they would like to eat? Do you list the menu and give them choices to check off? No, you expect them to enjoy the menu you have selected.

You are about to commit a social blunder, all in the name of being a conscientious hostess. You want your guests to enjoy themselves. But dinner at a wedding reception is not the same as dinner in a restaurant, where people can order what they please. It is a social occasion where they are served a meal selected by the parents of the bride and/or groom.

If you want to make sure everyone has just what they prefer, then work with the caterer to create a meal that has a little beef and a little chicken on it, plus vegetables. Or offer a buffet instead of a sit-down dinner. That would be much more acceptable than turning your wedding invitation into a menu.

SHOWERS OF BLESSINGS

Brides and grooms often invite guests to share their wedding memories, advice on a happy marriage, or to just record their best wishes. Many couples set up a video camera for guests to make recordings, but they often end up with a lot of drunken friends saying, "I love you, man." Here are some other less high-tech ideas.

- Set up a photo of the bride mounted in a frame and large mat without the glass. Guests "autograph" the mat with good wishes as the spirit moves them. Later the couple can use the mat around one of the wedding photos.

- Provide note cards and pens next to a beautifully decorated hatbox. Guests fill the hatbox with their best wishes.

(For more information on receptions, please see Budget, Invitations and Announcements, Music, Photography and Videography, Seating, and Second Wedding Style.)

Rehearsal Dinners

'Twas the Night Before the Wedding

*W*ith any performance, the players must rehearse. Then it is customary to entertain the cast and crew. So it goes with weddings. The "entertainment" is usually an informal, seated dinner, although a cocktail party, barbecue, picnic, or some other form of get-together is perfectly acceptable—including a formal dinner.

Who should be invited? Traditionally, the rehearsal dinner invitations went to the wedding party and their spouses, the bride's and groom's immediate families, and anyone else participating in the ceremony, including the parents of the flower girl and ring bearer. Often—especially in small towns—the officiant and spouse, the organist, and the soloist were also included. Today the guest list has expanded to include out-of-town family and guests as well.

Invitations should be issued two weeks before the wedding. If the party is very small, invitations may be issued verbally. But I believe in having things in writing. Even if guests are invited verbally, follow up with a written note so there can be no mistake about time and place.

Since rehearsal dinners are usually casual affairs, the invitations should reflect that. They may be printed or handwritten on plain cards with colorful borders that can be found in any stationery shop. The invitations can also reveal a theme, if there is one. For example, if the party is a barbecue, the invitations may have a western motif. If the rehearsal dinner is a picnic, the invitations may feature flowers.

The dinner is usually given by the groom's family, but it is perfectly acceptable if the bride's family or some other relative wishes to host the event. The hosts have final say-so on how elaborate (translation: expensive) the event will be. However, if the wedding is going to be ultraformal, the rehearsal dinner should not be beer and pretzels.

Couples often like to have their rehearsal dinner in a favorite restaurant, but it may be held at a club, hotel, or private home convenient to the wedding site. The festivities should not go on too late because the next day will be a busy one—and the smart bride and groom do not want their rehearsal dinner to overshadow the wedding!

Since the rehearsal dinner is more intimate than a wedding reception, this is the time to be emotional, with toasts welcoming the new son or daughter into the family and remembering deceased loved ones. It also is the time for siblings and friends to share their favorite embarrassing or slightly risqué tales about the bride and groom.

 ## What About the Kids?

If the couple has small children from a previous marriage, they may decide not to include the little ones at the rehearsal dinner. If the children do come, then the savvy bride or groom makes sure that a grandparent is on hand to help out. While moms and dads do want to include their children, they also want to be able to enjoy being a bride and groom.

If this is a second wedding, the couple's children may make toasts, if they choose, sharing funny stories or tender moments about their parents.

And it goes without saying that the couple should be sure to thank everyone.

IF THE BRIDE OR GROOM'S PARENTS ARE DIVORCED

As with other events involving divorced parents, planning a rehearsal dinner quickly becomes complicated. The traps are invitations—who issues them?—and seating—where should everyone sit when no one gets along? The same etiquette guidelines apply here as for weddings, so please see Invitations and Announcements, Receptions, and Seating for more details.

The invitations may be issued by parents and stepparents together. If the rehearsal party is formal, first and last names are used. If the dinner is a picnic or casual buffet, then first names are fine. Here are some examples, ranging from a formal engraved invitation to a printed invitation to a casual, handwritten note.

∞

Mr. and Mrs. Hal Wallace Berry [mother and stepfather of groom]
and
Mr. and Mrs. William Emmett Wood [father and stepmother of groom]
request the pleasure of your company
at a rehearsal dinner in honour of
Ms. Katherine Ann Hayes
and
Mr. Stephen William Wood

> *Friday, the eighth of June*
> *at half after seven o'clock*
> *Hedgerose Heights*
> *Tampa*

RSVP

∞

∞

> *Hal and Linda Berry*
> *and*
> *Will and Jean Wood*
> *request the pleasure of your company*
> *at a rehearsal dinner for*
> *Kathy and Steve*
> *Friday, June eighth*
> *at seven-thirty*
> *Hedgerose Heights*
> *Tampa*

RSVP
123-456-7890

∞

Dear Mary and Tommy,

Hal and I, along with Will and Jean Wood, would like for you to join us for dinner after the rehearsal for Steve and Kathy's wedding. Dinner will be at 7:30 P.M. June 8 at Hedgerose Heights, Steve and Kathy's favorite restaurant in Tampa. Please give me a call at 123-456-7890 to let me know whether you can be with us. We look forward to seeing you.

> *Best,*
> *Linda*

∞

Rehearsal dinners usually have assigned seating with place cards, but deciding where to seat divorced parents who do not get along need not be a problem. Simply put the bride, the groom, and the wedding party at a head table. Each set of parents then gets his and her separate table.

If the Bride or Groom Has Been Married

Although most second weddings are so small and informal that a rehearsal is not needed, couples may opt to spend the evening before their wedding with their immediate families (children, parents, and siblings) and a few close friends. Because they are usually paying for the wedding themselves, the couple usually gives the dinner, often at a favorite restaurant, but close friends may offer to host the get-together.

Invitations can be verbal or handwritten notes. Anything more elaborate is not needed.

Place cards should be used, and if the couple has divorced parents who do not get along, then care should be used to seat the feuding parents and their new spouses at opposite ends of the table.

Renewing Your Vows

"Let's Do It Again"

What happens when couples want to say, "I do" all over again? Reaffirmation of vows, more commonly known as "renewing our vows," has long been a rite whether in a church or in a synagogue.

These loving ceremonies—when a husband and wife promise they would marry each other all over again despite kids, bills, and mortgages—are held on a major anniversary, such as the twenty-fifth. Renewal services are simple affairs, often taking place during a regular service at the couple's church or synagogue. The couple wears their Sunday best, and their children may stand with them.

Some couples are using these religious ceremonies as an excuse to have a "second wedding," complete with bridesmaids, a fabulous gown, and lots of presents.

An exception may be made for the couple who married in a civil ceremony. They may have a church wedding within a year of their civil marriage. ∞

The reasons to hold a renewal service are as varied as the couple's choices of china. Maybe they eloped and didn't get to have "the wedding of our dreams." Perhaps the families couldn't afford an expensive wedding, and now they want a lavish affair with "all the trimmings." Some couples say their original wedding did not reflect their personalities, and that their parents used the event as a chance to pay back ten years worth of social obligations. Still other couples say they didn't have a good time at their own wedding. And at least one couple wanted to reenact their wedding because they didn't like the photographs from the first time!

Etiquette's answer is always the same: you are married. Wedding and renewal services are religious rites, not social rights. Couples who want to be the center of attention at a fabulous event should throw themselves a terrific anniversary party and dance the night away.

*A wanna-be bride writes: My husband and I want to renew our wedding vows on our tenth anniversary in two years. Our first wedding was held in our tiny living room, with just us, my mother-in-law, the minister, and two friends. It was terrible (my mother-in-law acted horribly), so we really want to "put on the hog" this time. Our budget is $12,000. Is it proper for us to put on an ultraformal wedding and reception for two hundred people? How should the invitations be worded? Is it proper for me to wear white? Who walks me down the aisle? Would a wedding consultant be of help? Can both silk and real flowers be used? I've been told that I should wear a sophisticated gown, but my dream dress is a full-skirted chiffon delight. PS—My mother-in-law and I are now best friends. —*WANTS TO BE A BRIDE AGAIN

DEAR WANTS: If you can put on an ultraformal wedding for only $12,000, you must be a financial wizard. Weddings today cost far more, and the fancier they are, the more expensive they get.

A vow renewal is *not* another wedding, especially not "the wedding I've always dreamed of." It is a simple religious ceremony usually performed on a couple's major anniversary, such as the twentieth or twenty-fifth. The couple wears their Sunday-going-to-meeting clothes.

But you can have a fabulous anniversary party. Wear a big-skirted chiffon dress and dance the night away. But forget about wedding consultants and walking down the aisle like a bride.

PS—I'm glad you and your mother-in-law have patched things up.

*A wanna-be bride writes: My husband and I are having a reaffirmation of our vows this year. I would like to know if someone is supposed to "give" me away. My parents are divorced, and my father has very limited contact with my siblings and me. He has shown no interest in our second "big day" and thinks the whole idea ridiculous. My mother and her significant other (who treats me like a daughter) have taken on the majority of the expenses. I would like to have my mother "give" me away, but I know that my father's side of the family won't see it that way. They blame her for the divorce. I want to know what is the correct thing to do so I won't step on any toes. —*ONCE WAS NOT ENOUGH

DEAR ONCE: While I can't say I agree wholeheartedly with your father, I do think the idea of passing a second wedding off as "renewing our vows" is rather silly. A reaffirmation ceremony is a simple, private service often held right after Sunday church or in the minister's study with only the couple and their family present, usually on a major anniversary.

This is a chance for couples to rededicate their lives to each other and to God, not the opportunity for the bride to wear a big, white dress and have the wedding she never had. My advice is to forget being given away—I think you already have been.

> "Chains do not hold a marriage together. It is threads, hundreds of tiny threads, which sew people together through the years."
> —*Simone Signoret, author*

*A sister of the bride writes: Is there a proper way of going about renewing your vows? My sister and her husband want to do this for their twentieth anniversary, but what they are planning is an actual wedding, complete with attendants, two hundred guests, a reception, and her walking down the aisle. They're not so much renewing their vows as giving themselves something they didn't have the first time: a big wedding. I tried to steer her toward an anniversary party, but she said that everything she's ever read about it says you can do whatever you want. I always thought that renewing your vows was a very personal thing, that you have only family and maybe a few friends, with a party afterward. Am I wrong in thinking this? Is my sister correct when she says etiquette allows her to do whatever she wishes? She has asked for my help in this, but I feel uncomfortable about this. —*CONCERNED

DEAR CONCERNED: Your sister is planning a wedding, not a reaffirmation ceremony. But I don't think she is going to want to hear you tell her that she is being tacky. She possibly will be angry and resentful.

You may show her this book, or you may opt—in the interest of peace in the family—to keep a low profile. I just wish I knew where she gets the idea that "etiquette allows her to do whatever she wishes." Many bridal magazines push this concept in order to help their advertisers sell more wedding products, but etiquette never condones lavish displays of selfishness.

*A wanna-be bride writes: My husband and I were married in a small civil service. We agreed that on our fifteenth wedding anniversary we would have a large ceremony and reception and even a honeymoon. I don't know what is proper for this type of service, from what to wear to what to serve at the reception. —*WAITING

DEAR WAITING: You need to consult with your minister about renewing your vows. Most denominations have special ceremonies and guidelines for this.

As for your "reception" afterward, please give it its proper name: wedding-anniversary party.

*A **wanna-be bride** writes: My husband and I would like to renew our vows. We are only twenty-three and twenty-four years old, but we have been married for three years and have two children. We got married when I was six months pregnant with our first son. I didn't want a wedding. It didn't seem right to me. So on our fifth anniversary, we want to have a wedding.*

I'm confused about the do's and don'ts. Should I wear white or ivory? Would it be wrong for my two brothers to give me away? What about invitations? How many attendants should we have? I thought two each would be enough.

*People think I am crazy, but shouldn't every woman have the wedding of her dreams? And have those memories, instead of having memories of being six months pregnant and going to a justice of the peace? At least we knew the j.p., so it wasn't that bad. —*TWO-TIMING IN TEXAS

DEAR TWO-TIMING: Every woman having the "wedding of her dreams" is a nice sentiment but not very practical. Sometimes there are financial restraints. (By the way, who is to pay for this one? We doubt your parents want the honor.)

A renewal-of-vows ceremony is usually held at the twentieth or twenty-fifth anniversary mark, to celebrate a couple's affirmation of their commitment to each other. You need to check with your officiant. Many denominations have regulations regarding a renewal-of-vows service. Some churches will allow a second wedding (which is what you are proposing) when the couple was married in a civil service, usually twelve months earlier. But there may be restrictions on the size and type of wedding.

The proper way to celebrate is with a small, dignified service similar to one that would be acceptable for a second marriage. Don't try to undo time.

∞ "Love seems to be the swiftest, but it is the slowest of all growths. No man or woman really knows what perfect love is until they have been married a quarter of a century."
—*Mark Twain*

Your husband and you would issue handwritten invitations. The simple ceremony could be followed by a lavish anniversary party. But forget trying to have bridesmaids, a veil, and the other trappings of a wedding. Wear a smart suit or a dressy dress in cream or ivory. No veil please, and a corsage or small bouquet is appropriate.

You and your husband should have no more than one attendant each, if any, and no, you do not need to be given away. You already have been.

Rings and Other Jewelry

Precious Memories

*J*ewelry, particularly if it is valuable or heirloom, can become an issue in divorce and remarriage. Here are some guidelines.

BROKEN ENGAGEMENTS

If the engagement was broken by the bride, the engagement ring should be returned to the groom and his family, particularly if it has sentimental or historic value. Any family heirloom pieces, such as great-grandma's cameo, also should be returned.

If the future bridegroom breaks the engagement, allowing the bride to keep the ring is the gracious thing to do. This is something the two of them should work out. If the bride keeps her engagement ring, she may wish to have the stone reset.

In some instances, the bride's family has sued to keep rings and other jewelry, particularly if the family had already incurred expenses while planning the wedding.

DIVORCE

The husband and wife retain their rings but no longer wear them. In many cases, the rings are put away to be given to their children when the time is right. Again, a woman may decide to reset the stones as a piece of jewelry that she can enjoy without being reminded of the failed marriage.

If rings or other jewelry are heirlooms from the husband's family, a divorced woman may set them aside for her children. If there were no children, the couple may decide to include the jewelry in their divorce settlement. Heirloom jewelry is also something that can be covered in a prenuptial agreement.

REMARRIAGE

When a man or woman who has been married before marries again, the couple may exchange rings just as in a first-time marriage. However, it is considered poor taste for a man to give his new wife an engagement ring worn by a previous wife. Instead, that jewelry should be put away for his children. This also ensures that the jewelry—and the peace—will remain in his family in case of another divorce. However, if there are no children and the new wife loves the older jewelry, he may present it to her if he wishes. Again, this issue should be covered in a prenuptial agreement, particularly if there are children.

A bride writes: My little brother is six years old and will be the ring bearer. Does he give the rings to the groom or to the best man? —RING BEARER'S SISTER

DEAR SIS: The rings he carries are only "pretend" rings. You don't want to trust him with the real things, which should be safely in the best man's pocket.

Seating

Who Goes Where?

$\mathscr{E}$xtended families and their multiples of parents and stepparents are the bane of well-meaning couples who want only to "do what's right." Trying to fit today's families into yesterday's traditions leaves brides and grooms seriously considering elopement. Put away the ladders. There are ways to compromise.

AT THE CEREMONY

The front row on the right is reserved for the mother and father of the groom while the left front row is for the parents of the bride (this is reversed in a Conservative or Orthodox Jewish ceremony). When parents are divorced, the custodial parent (usually the mother) gets the first row while the other parent sits one or two rows back. If the relationships are particularly acrimonious, seat the father and his new wife toward the rear of the church—well out of striking distance.

Couples should work out the seating from these basics. For more information, please see The Ceremony.

A bride writes: My divorced parents, who have remarried, are on friendly terms, so will it be OK to seat them together in the front row? —DAUGHTER OF DIVORCE

DEAR DAUGHTER: If they agree, seat them all together.

A bride writes: My fiancé's mother and father are divorced, and his father has remarried. How do we go about seating his parents? Where does his stepmother sit? I feel closer to the stepmother, and I don't think these two ladies get along too well. —CONFUSED

DEAR CONFUSED: Your fiancé's mom has the place of honor in the first row on the right. She need not be all by her lonesome, however. Her parents, another relative, or her escort may sit there as well.

Your fiancé's father and stepmother may sit there, too, if the families are congenial. If not, your fiancé's father and his wife should sit in the second row—or farther back.

A bride writes: My parents are divorced, and my mother has remarried. I have asked my brother to escort me down the aisle, so where should my father sit? Should he sit in the pew behind my mother with my grandparents? —SEATING CHART

DEAR SEATING: If your parents get along, he sits in the row behind your mother. If theirs was a particularly wretched divorce, it may be prudent to seat him several rows farther back.

A bride writes: My parents are divorced, and my father has been out of my life for twenty-one years by his choice. Needless to say, my mother will attend our wedding without an escort. How is she brought into the church and the reception? May I use an usher as her escort? We have four ushers and three bridesmaids in our wedding. —Looking Out for Mom

Dear Looking: Your mother will be escorted into the church just as the groom's mother would be: by a groomsman or usher. It would be a nice touch to ask a groomsman who is related to you to do the honors of seeing her settled into her seat on the first row. Then he would return to the back of the church to walk down the aisle with the rest of the wedding party.

At the reception, your mother will be greeting guests in the receiving line so she will not need an escort. The line should be made up of you, your fiancé, and your mothers. His father need not take part.

A bride writes: I have questions I can't find answers for, or the answers I find, I don't like. Both sets of parents are divorced, and my parents are not at all friendly. My father has remarried. My fiancé's parents are quite compatible. Who sits where? I've been told that my father must sit in the third row with his new wife. Does he have to? My stepmother has helped me plan the wedding, and we are somewhat close. Where does my stepfamily sit in the church? Who comes into the church in what order when it comes to mothers, fathers, attendants, and ushers? —Parental Problems

Dear Parental: You may not like the answers this time either, but that is why rules of etiquette have evolved: to show you what to do in social situations. You don't have to follow them if you don't like them, but you risk stirring up more familial ill will by acting capriciously. Everyone knows what he or she is supposed to do when you follow the traditional guidelines found in etiquette books. When you do it "your way," no one understands.

Your mother traditionally has the place of honor on the first row on the bride's side, even if she has nothing else to do with your wedding. Your father would sit with his wife and the rest of your stepfamily in the second or third row, behind your mother.

Your stepmother would not be part of the "mothers' processional," which actually is not an official part of the wedding, into the church, but you can have her seated about ten minutes before the wedding starts. After your fiancé's mother and then your mother are seated, the wedding begins with your ushers coming down the aisle first.

A bride writes: My father, who is divorced from my mother, will not be giving me away. Do I just have him there as a guest or is there a special place he and his girlfriend should sit? Is there a special job he should do? —Not Daddy's Girl

Dear Not: The traditional job of the father of the bride is to escort her and to pay the bills. Since you have already taken care of these functions, your father doesn't have to worry about anything except having a good time.

He and his girlfriend would sit in the row behind your mother, a rather special spot, unless your parents do not get along. Then he and his guest sit farther back.

A bride writes: Where would a divorced grandfather and his new wife sit at his grandson's wedding? Where would his first wife sit? —Perplexed

Dear Perplexed: In some families, divorced grandparents can peacefully coexist on the same row, right behind the mother of the groom. But relations are not so cordial in some families. In those cases, grandmother takes the second row or sits in the first row with her son or daughter, while grandfather and his new bride sit farther back.

A bride writes: My father, with whom I've lived all my life until a few years ago, has been married three times. He divorced my mother when I was three, and although she lives on the West Coast, we keep in touch. My stepmother, who raised me, divorced my dad when I was in college. She, too, keeps in touch. Now my dad and mothers are all remarried. When my sisters were married, seating arrangements left everyone with an uncomfortable feeling. Where should everyone sit to feel equally important? Thank you. —PARENT TRAPPED

DEAR TRAPPED: Unfortunately, a wedding is not a democracy. Everyone can't and everyone won't feel equally important because no matter how much you love them all, some are more important than others.

Your mother *is* your mother, so that makes her important. She will sit in the first row on the left-hand side, with her current husband.

Your father will be escorting you down the aisle, we presume, so that makes *him* important. After escorting you, he takes his place with his current wife. She should be sitting in the row behind your mother or behind your grandparents and other relatives on your mother's side.

Your former stepmother who raised you is technically no longer any relation to you. Officially, she should be seated outside the family section, but on the bride's side. But because you obviously love her, have her seated in your family section (but not in the same row as your father). She will understand the honor. You might also provide her with flowers to wear. (Please see Flowers.)

A bride writes: Where do you seat the parents if your mother has remarried and your father has not? My father will give me away, but my mother and stepfather will be attending. —WORRIED

DEAR WORRIED: You follow the same procedure described in the previous letter. Your mother and her current husband would claim the first row on the bride's side. Your father, after he and your mother have given you away, would sit behind them or behind other family members on your mother's side. (Please see Escorting the Bride.)

A bride writes: I have a mother and a stepdad, who by the way, are financing the wedding, plus a father and a stepmother who are separated but plan to attend the wedding as a couple. How should they be seated? I also have grandparents, some of whom are divorced and remarried. The front pews are tiny in this church and may not seat everyone (tempers may be short, too). —CAUGHT IN THE MIDDLE

DEAR CAUGHT: Oh, dear . . . you don't think they need to be separated like naughty children, do you? If there is room and they get along, your mother, father, and their spouses may share the front row on the left-hand side. If this is too much togetherness, your mother and stepfather (and her mother, if you desire) should be in the front row, with your dad and his separated wife just behind. Beginning with your mother's mother, grandparents should fill in from the third row back.

You might tell them of your arrangements in advance, citing the desire to make sure everyone is comfortable on those tiny pews.

A mother of the bride writes: I am divorced and have not remarried. Is it always customary to seat the divorced father and his new family directly behind the mother of the bride? May my mother sit with me? —BRIDE'S MOM

DEAR MOM: It depends on how well you and your ex get along. If you are friends, he and his new family may sit in the row behind you. If you aren't, put them farther back. And, yes, your mother may sit with you.

AT THE RECEPTION

Etiquette has solved the problem of what to do with divorced parents at the reception by giving everyone separate tables. If they get along, divorced parents may share a table. The following are the traditional arrangements:

The Bride's Table

The following folks sit at the bride's table: bride, groom, attendants, and their spouses. The officiant and his or her spouse also sit here if they attend the reception and if they are close in age to the couple. The bride sits on the groom's right. The bride's table is always served by waiters, even if the wedding dinner is buffet style, and the bride is served first.

The Parents' Table

The bride's mother sits opposite the bride's father. The groom's father always sits in the place of honor—to the right of the bride's mother, who is hostess. The groom's mother always sits in the place of honor—to the right of the bride's father, who is host. The rest of the table is filled in with the honored guests, close relatives, grandparents, officiant and spouse (optional), and so forth.

A bride writes: How do we set up the seating at the reception? Do the families sit at the same table or at separate tables? Do the bridesmaids and groomsmen all sit at the same table? Do the bride and groom sit alone together?
—TAKING A SEAT

Place cards need not be used except on the tables for the bride and groom and their parents. ∞

DEAR TAKING: The wedding party usually is seated together, while the families frequently preside over their own tables. The bride and groom join the wedding party, but in some cultures, the newlyweds are installed at a small, romantic table for two. A groom who married a woman from Mexico, where this is a tradition, jokingly told me he thought no one in her family liked him when he and his bride were ushered to their table for two.

The Parents' Table When Parents Are Divorced

Divorced parents are not usually seated at the same table, although if they get along, they may be. An easy way to handle this problem is to assign each divorced parent (and new spouse) a separate table for family and friends.

At the Rehearsal Dinner and Dinner Parties

At dinners honoring the couple before the marriage, including the rehearsal dinner, the bride and the future groom are always seated together. If either the bride's or the groom's parents are divorced and do not get along, the parents should be seated at separate tables. However, if the divorced parents are amicable and everyone wants to sit together, the following seating charts may apply:

1. **Bride's parents divorced, mother remarried:** officiant's spouse (optional), officiant (optional), groom's mother, bride's father, maid of honor, groom, bride, best man, bride's mother, bride's stepfather, groom's father

2. **Bride's parents divorced, father remarried:** officiant's spouse (optional), officiant (optional), bride's stepmother, bride's father, maid of honor, groom, bride, best man, bride's mother, groom's father, groom's stepfather

3. **Groom's parents divorced, mother remarried:** groom's stepfather, groom's mother, bride's father, maid of honor, groom, bride, best man, bride's mother, groom's father, officiant (optional), officiant's spouse (optional), and so forth.

4. **Groom's parents divorced, father remarried:** officiant's spouse (optional), officiant (optional), groom's mother, bride's father, maid of

honor, groom, bride, best man, bride's mother, groom's father, groom's stepmother

5. **All of the parents divorced, all remarried:** bride's stepmother, bride's father, groom's stepmother, groom's father, maid of honor, groom, bride, best man, bride's mother, bride's stepfather, groom's stepmother, groom's father.

Second Wedding Style

What's Proper or How to Marry Again Without Offending Amy Vanderbilt

*O*nce upon a time, etiquette decreed that second weddings had to be so low-key that a woman marrying again might wonder if she had actually gone through a wedding ceremony. No white dress and certainly no veil. Some churches even banned music at second weddings, and couples who allowed their children from another marriage to participate in the ceremony were considered gauche. Divorce was a shameful act in those days, and society did not want to acknowledge that a bride had ever been deflowered, much less pregnant.

Today, brides are being told that "anything goes!" Wear white if your heart is "pure." Have *beaucoups de* bridesmaids. Register at all your favorite stores. And do everything you didn't get to do the first time around.

This leaves people confused. Everyone has his or her idea of what is "correct," and they don't always jibe. For example, your next mother-in-law may not be hip to the latest changes in wedding etiquette; she may still think it is a scandal for a second-time bride to wear white.

How much tradition to flout is a decision you and your fiancé will have to make. Having the wedding you've always wanted may be much more important to you than what Miss Manners calls "the snigger factor." No matter what you do, people will giggle and criticize.

While I don't agree with the "anything goes!" theory—after all, not everyone you know will want to ante up for yet another wedding gift—I do think second weddings should be a cause for celebration and rejoicing. Just do it tastefully.

The key here is moderation with the emphasis on family. Bridesmaids are acceptable, just not as many of them as the first time the bride trekked to the altar. And children, of course, should be an important part of the ceremony.

This time around, the bride and groom should find themselves having more fun. After all, they've had practice.

A bride writes: This is a very delicate situation. I am thirty-eight years old and have three marriages behind me. All three ended in divorce, two of them because of abuse. Now I am a converted Christian about to become engaged to a wonderful Christian man who has never been married. I know his mother will want to have a large wedding. I have never had a large wedding. This marriage will be very special since I have been asking God for a special mate. I don't want to deprive my fiancé just because I made so many mistakes in the past. I have a pale pink and white gown with a train on layaway—without a veil, of course. Would it be in bad taste to continue planning such an elaborate wedding? I have ladies—married, Christian ladies—who want to be in the wedding. What should I do? —A NEW LIFE

DEAR NEW LIFE: You may be depriving your future mother-in-law of a large wedding, but we doubt your fiancé will mind. Somehow men just don't seem to get as caught up in all the folderol of a wedding as women do. So let's leave him out of it.

You do not specify how "large" a wedding you and your future mother-in-law are planning. A quiet ceremony in front of family and close friends with a few attendants—not a cast of thousands, please!—is perfectly acceptable for multiple weddings and for older brides, categories that describe your situation—although we think that by a fourth wedding the number of attendants should be pared down to one.

As for dress, you should be thinking elegant evening dress or suit instead of a wedding gown with a train.

You also should consider the guidelines of your church. Some have rules against large ceremonies for divorced persons. Some even ban music.

Since Christ has become such a big part of your lives together, put the emphasis on the religious aspects of your wedding ceremony, not the secular ones.

A bride writes: I was married before. I was eighteen and it was a courthouse ceremony with no frills. I was married in another state, and no one but close family and my fiancé even knows it took place. Now I am twenty-six. My fiancé and I want a wedding with all the pomp and circumstance. His parents will be paying for it, and his mother really wants to go all out. He is her only child. Would this be too presumptuous of me? Should I pay for a mistake I made in my past by not having the wedding of my dreams? A man who has been married before can have a big wedding. Why should a woman be penalized? —PAST REGRETS

DEAR PAST: Good question. Society's guides have not kept up with society's ways. The guidelines tend to reflect an era before the days when one in every two marriages ends in divorce, many after only a year.

But there are practical considerations. Brides' parents who have spent a bundle of money on first weddings only to see them dissolve shouldn't be expected to pay again, nor should guests be expected to produce present after present as a woman—or a man—racks up a string of weddings.

And let's not forget the most important consideration: the seriousness and symbolism of those wedding vows. Too many people take "for better or worse" very casually, spending more time on what the wedding will look like than on what it will mean.

Some wedding experts advise second- and third-time brides that they can have the wedding of their dreams, white gown and all, as long as their hearts are "pure." Hokey as it sounds, we can go along with that, although we would advise against having the most formal of weddings with the longest of veils.

So, have a big wedding, but only if you promise that you will spend as much time thinking about how your life will be with this man as you do about what your dress will look like.

A bride writes: This will be my third marriage and my fiancé's second, but neither of us has ever had a real *wedding with a minister instead of a justice of the peace. We would really love to have a big wedding and reception. We are paying for everything ourselves. I want to do it right. What about etiquette and attire? What about groomsmen and attendants?* —THIRD TIME'S THE CHARM

DEAR THIRD: Forgive me, but just what is a *real* wedding? The vows you took the first two times counted just as much—well, maybe almost as much—as the ones you will take the third time. Like you, we too hope that "the third time is the charm." You have been married, albeit by justices of the peace. By all means, do it again. Let's hope practice makes perfect.

If you are having a religious service, you will also need to consult with your clergy person to see just how much pomp and circumstance your church will allow, but keep it simple. No long, white "princess for a day" gown with flounces and a train. No veil. Just one honor attendant. Restraint is the key for a tasteful third wedding.

A bride writes: This will be my fiancé's first wedding, but my second. He is thirty-one, an only child, close to his parents, self-employed, and a rising politician. I was married in another state for just six years and have two sons, ages seven and two. Because of my fiancé's "status," we thought it would be proper to have a fairly large wedding and want to send two hundred invitations. Would it be proper for me to have only one honor attendant, my fiancé's mother? Do I need to have more if he is having three or four groomsmen (including the best man)? We are trying to incorporate my sons into the ceremony. I have thought about having one or both of them walk me down the aisle. We plan to have an evening wedding, and although I will be in a floor-length gown and Steve will be in a tuxedo, we don't want it to be a truly formal wedding. Will guests assume it is black tie because it will be at 6 P.M.? We plan to have cake, punch, nuts, and mints at the reception, even though this is an evening wedding. Do guests expect more? Do we need to set up tables or will chairs suffice? I want an evening wedding but without the hassle of a sit-down reception. —NIGHT-TIME BRIDE

DEAR BRIDE: Your wedding is neither fish nor fowl. Your problem is that you want a formal wedding without going to the trouble—and expense—of a formal affair. What you are planning will leave your guests wondering why you tried to have an evening wedding "on the cheap."

A six o'clock wedding is a formal affair, and guests recognize it as tuxedo time. But the reception you have in mind is more appropriate for a more casual afternoon wedding. If you are so concerned about "status," you will look quite silly. Your guests will wonder why they got all dressed up.

In view of your previous marriage, why not have a more casual afternoon ceremony? You can still invite hordes of potential voters, er, guests. You can still include your sons in the ceremony. You can still have only one attendant (although we think the mother of the groom is a strange choice). You can still serve nuts and mints.

You will not have built up your guests' expectations, and you will have squashed any comments related to the inappropriateness of *your* flashy second wedding.

A bride writes: I am twenty-nine years old and have been married three times. I have been asked that question again—"Will you marry me?"—only this time my fiancé has a job. The wedding, which will be small and simple, will actually be my first wedding. I have heard these no-nos: no veils, no pearls, no lace, no white dress, no invitations. Please, what advice do you have for me?
—ONE MORE TIME

DEAR ONE MORE: My advice is "good luck." Obviously after three strikes, you are not out, but a wedding with all the trimmings is out of the ballpark for a bride who will be marrying for the fourth time— no matter how small her previous weddings.

A wedding with lots of bridesmaids, a Princess Diana dress, and a long train is reserved for the innocent young. You do not fall into that category. Your wedding should follow the guidelines for any second or subsequent marriage: small, quiet, and tasteful. That means a dressy suit (OK, it can be ivory), a hat (no veil), and a corsage or small bouquet. There is no reason why you cannot wear pearls.

Second weddings are small enough that guests are invited by hand-written notes, which is quite elegant.

Many couples marrying for the second time (or more) often like to have blowout receptions after a simple wedding service (which I much prefer to a large, tacky wedding ceremony), but an elegant dinner is very appropriate.

A bride writes: My fiancé and I both were previously engaged, although never married, and had broken off our respective engagements prior to meeting one another. We plan a formal wedding. I plan to wear an elaborate gown with a train and veil. I own a house, and my fiancé will move in with me five months prior to the wedding after he completes his military service in another state.

Would any of these factors preclude the kind of wedding we are planning? It seemed foolish for my fiancé to rent an apartment for only five months. —ROOMMATES

DEAR ROOMMATES: When it comes to determining how lavish a wedding one can have, previous engagements and living arrangements don't count. Prior weddings, and the size of one's pocketbook, do. More than one bride has worn a virginal white gown even though she can't claim the label herself.

A bride writes: My situation is a slightly complicated one. I plan on getting married in about a year. Before, I married very young—in my teens—in a simple wedding with only two bridesmaids and no elaborate gown. For my second wedding, I want to go all out. I want a beautiful gown and veil. I want a few bridesmaids, ushers, everything. I feel that I missed out when I married the first time. I want my second wedding to be extra special. Would it be considered really "taboo" for wanting all that? Should I have all the extras? A long, white gown? A veil? I really want them though. I am confused, totally confused. —DREAMING OF A WHITE WEDDING

DEAR DREAMING: Weddings are first and foremost religious ceremonies, and no matter how unhappy or unfortunate a first marriage has been, a woman cannot pretend that it never took place. Before going

 It Was All a Mistake. Let's Get Married Again!

Some couples who divorce decide that love is better the second time around and decide to remarry each other. Invitations are not sent for remarriage ceremonies. Friends and family are informed of the event verbally. The ceremony is private, and no announcements are sent to newspapers. Needless to say, the couple does not have attendants, and the bride does not wear an elaborate gown.

any further, you should confer with your officiant about the elaborateness of your second wedding. He or she might not permit a large wedding with oodles of attendants and a wedding march.

As for dress, you may wear a "bridey" dress, but don't wear pure white or a veil. These are symbols of purity and virginity. Opt instead for ivory or a gown with pastel touches. Your headdress should be a hat or flowers, and wear a corsage or carry a small bouquet.

Showers and Parties

Getting Together

$\mathcal{W}$omen once saw weddings as a golden opportunity to entertain their friends or their friends' daughters. No one gives bridge or canasta or "Coke" parties for brides anymore—can't you just see today's career women dropping everything at the office to spend an afternoon playing cards or drinking soft drinks with "the girls"? But part of the fun of getting married is all of the other festivities surrounding a wedding. Your friends and those of your parents will want to honor you with parties.

Entertaining for a bridal couple today is often limited to coed showers, his-and-her bachelor parties, a rehearsal dinner, and perhaps an engagement party. But hosts and hostesses should be more creative. Couples may be given dinner parties, picnics, barbecues, dessert parties, cocktail parties, or pool parties. Parties for the bride might include teas and coffees, luncheons, or a mother-daughter tea. In some parts of the country, the bride's mother hosts a trousseau tea so women friends may see the wedding presents, including the bride's lingerie.

If a bride has a great many friends who want to entertain for her, she may wish to ask some of them to go in together on a party. With input from her mother, the bride prepares the guest lists, which usually consist of family and friends who will be invited to the wedding.

TO SHOWER OR NOT TO SHOWER?

A shower basically is a party where guests are expected to bring gifts to help the couple furnish their new home. Most are women-only—teas, coffees, or brunches—but many couples have at least one coed shower, which is usually a cocktail party.

Guests usually are asked to bring gifts to fit the "theme" of the shower, usually held about three or four weeks before the wedding. Themes usually include kitchen, bath, lingerie, garden, bar and wine cellar, gadget, or miscellaneous. Invitations should specify what kind of shower and any other pertinent information to help guests, such as "The color of Jim and Sue's kitchen is yellow." Some hostesses even go so far as to put the name of the store where the couple is registered on the shower invitation.

Some showers are "twenty-four-hour showers." Guests are assigned an hour of the day or night, say 8 A.M., and expected to bring a gift that would be appropriate at that hour of the day, such as a coffeemaker. Guests assigned odd hours get pretty creative!

It is traditional to "shower" a first-time bride with gifts for her trousseau or her new home, even if she has a closet full of designer clothes and a house full of furniture, but a second-time bride may also be showered. The second-time bride who already has a kitchen full of gadgets may prefer a shower that focuses on personal gifts for her, such as lingerie or bath products.

The guidelines for showers are the same whether or not the bride has been married before.

• **The maid or matron of honor usually is the hostess.** Although a cousin of the bride may act as hostess, having a close family member give a shower makes the bride look greedy. Friends of the bride or of her mother or the groom's mother also may give showers.

• **The guest list should include the bride's mother, the groom's mother, and the couple's grandmothers, sisters, aunts, cousins, and friends.** If relationships are amicable, the bride may invite stepmothers and stepsisters, but their presence is not required. The same guidelines apply to coed showers.

• **Each guest should be invited to only one shower, no matter how many you have.** Showers are unabashed grabs for goodies, so it's impolite to hit anyone up more than once—unless, of course, your sisters want to attend them all.

• **Guests invited to a shower must be invited to the wedding.**

• **Showers may include both sexes.**

• **A bride should not have more than two or three showers.** Any more and the bride looks greedy. If you have lots of friends who want to give showers for you, ask them to have another kind of party, such as a tea, cocktail party, or barbecue, where gifts are not required. You can also consider asking friends who want to have parties for you to go in together as hostesses.

A Special Thanks

Don't forget to thank your hostess with a short letter and flowers or a bottle of wine sent the next day.

• **The bridesmaids should be invited to all showers, although they need not attend each one.** If the shower is for the bride and groom, the groomsmen should be invited as well.

• **The bride thanks each guest at the party, yet follows up with short thank-you notes.**

A bride writes: *Do you invite out-of-state wedding guests to a shower if you know they cannot come? Is this being greedy for gifts or thoughtful?* —SHOWER POWER

DEAR SHOWER: If you know they can't come, yet you invite them anyway, yes, it does look greedy—even though you may be attempting to be courteous.

By the way, guests who cannot attend a shower are not obligated to send gifts.

If I could change anything about my wedding, I would have planned at least one women-only shower instead of two coed showers. I attended a shower/brunch for my friend where the guests were women ages twenty-five to eighty-one. We had the best time! Such energy came from these ladies who were successful career women and wives and mothers! I realized how important and empowering it is for women to share rituals. ∞

Stepparents

Handling Those Sticky Situations

*D*ivorced parents can wreck a wedding, but stepparents have been known to pull dirty tricks, too. At the marriage of her stepson, one woman in California deliberately waited until the mothers had been seated before making her entrance with the father of the groom. The stepmother wanted the honor of being the last "mother" seated.

She tried to pull the same stunt again at her second stepson's wedding, but, having been warned in advance, the bride was too quick for her. "Seat them at the back of the church," the bride told the wedding coordinator.

How can a bride or groom avoid trouble? Talk with your parents and stepparents beforehand and let them know that you expect them to act like grownups and put aside any animosities for the wedding.

The Gracious Stepparent's Ten Commandments or How to Earn the Undying Loyalty of Your Family

- Insist that you and your spouse contribute financially to the wedding, especially if he is father of the bride.
- Do not expect any control over the wedding planning.
- Do not pout when your lovingly given advice is ignored. In fact, don't give any unless asked!
- Do offer your assistance to the bride and her mother in running errands or handling mundane tasks.
- Do not fret when your spouse is asked to pose for family photographs that include his or her ex.
- Do not insist that your name be on the invitations, even when it should be.
- Do not insist on standing in the receiving line, even if you should.
- Do not insist that your children be part of the wedding ceremony, even when they should be.
- Do host a party for the couple, but do not upstage festivities hosted by the father or mother.
- Do not try to upstage the parents in any way by dressing or acting to draw attention to yourself.

A bride writes: How should my stepmother enter the church, and where should she and my father sit? How should the engagement announcement read? I want

Remember

To keep your marriage brimming
With love in the marriage cup,
Whenever you're wrong, admit it;
Whenever you're right, shut up!
—*Ogden Nash*

my mother's name to be used even though she is deceased, and I would prefer that my stepmother's name not be used. I care for her, but she did not raise me. —Missing Mom

Dear Missing: Like the other guests, your stepmother is seated by an usher about ten or fifteen minutes before the wedding begins. If you do not have grandmothers you would like seated in the first row on the left, she may sit there.

After you and your father reach the front, he passes your hand to your groom. Then he retires to sit with your stepmother.

Engagement and wedding announcements for the newspapers should carry both of your parents' names: Mr. William Edward Linden and the late Mrs. Shirley Morrison Linden.

Since your mother is deceased, her name would not appear on your wedding invitations. And because you and your fiancé are giving the wedding, you need not list your father or your stepmother either:

The honour of your presence
is requested at the marriage of
Miss Shirley Jane Linden
and
Mr. Henry Dawes Williams
[and so forth]

For more information, please see Invitations and Announcements and Seating.

A bride writes: Until recently, my father and I had not been very close. My parents are divorced, and I grew up with my mother. My father has not offered to contribute financially to my wedding. My mom and stepdad will pay for everything, and my brother is going to walk me down the aisle. How do my dad and stepmother fit in? —Muddled Bride

DEAR MUDDLED: Your father and his wife are treated like honored guests. They should receive an invitation, not be mentioned on it. If your parents are amicable, your dad and stepmom should be seated in the second row behind your mother and stepfather. If not, they should be seated farther back. Your father and his wife do not participate in the receiving line at the reception, but do get a photograph of them with you.

A stepmother of the bride writes: My stepdaughter will be married in April. Her father and I will be giving both the wedding and the reception, although her mother will be present. I have the following questions:

- *How should the invitations read?*
- *What are the seating arrangements at the church?*

I appreciate your reply, as I am anxious for this day to be perfect for my step-daughter. —MISSISSIPPI STEPMOM

DEAR STEPMOM: After hearing so often from feuding stepfamilies, it's wonderful to come across someone who has put the bride's happiness first! We wish you all the best. The invitations should read:

Mr. and Mrs. Winston Kemper Leake
requests the honour of your presence
at the marriage of his daughter [if appropriate, "their" may be used]
Madeline Martine
[and so forth]

The bride's mother (and her husband, if she has remarried) should be seated in the first row on the left. Her side of the family would sit directly behind her. You would be seated behind them, and your husband—after he escorts his daughter—sits with you.

If there are bad feelings between the bride's divorced parents, you and your husband would sit two or three rows farther back. If the bride grew up in your home, the order is reversed. You and your husband sit on the first row, and the mother of the bride and her husband sit farther back.

*A bride writes: My fiancé's parents are divorced, and each has been remarried for some time. He lived with his grandparents for eleven years. They raised him, so he considers them his parents. He wants his grandfather to be his best man and his grandmother to sit in his mother's place during the ceremony and the reception. Is this inappropriate because his parents are still living? Where would his parents and stepparents sit? —*DIVORCE DILEMMA

DEAR DILEMMA: Biology may make someone a mother or a father, but they are not always "parents." If your fiancé considers his grandparents his "parents," that's all that matters. Your fiancé's asking his grandfather to be his best man is a lovely gesture, and his grandmother should sit in the first row. She should be escorted into the wedding just as the mother of the groom would be. She is followed by your mother, who is the last person to be seated.

Your fiancé's parents and stepparents may be seated in the second row. If any of them do not get along, put more distance between them.

For more information, please see Invitations and Announcements and Seating.

Tacky Mistakes
to Avoid

"Was My Face Red!"

*N*o matter how many times you marry, the following just isn't done.

- Enclosing your bridal registry list in your wedding invitations
- Specifying "Adults Only" on your wedding invitations
- The groom's serenading the bride during the ceremony, or vice versa, unless you have voices like Sting and Linda Ronstadt
- Asking guests to contribute toward a) your mortgage, b) your honeymoon, or c) your wedding expenses
- "Treating" your guests to a cash bar at the reception
- Displaying gifts at the wedding reception
- Becoming engaged before your divorce is final

A bride writes: May we state on the invitations that "Only your prayers and attendance requested. No gifts, please"? —GOOD INTENTIONS

DEAR INTENTIONS: Don't even begin to think about putting "No gifts" on the invitations. Even though you mean well, a gift is no longer a gift unless it is freely given. Your friends and family will want to recognize the solemnity of this moment in your lives with gifts they hope you will enjoy and cherish. Please give them the opportunity to do so. (For more information, please see Gifts.)

> ∞ "It's your wedding, and you should do what you want to do. And I'm sure that what you will want to do is to offend as few people as possible."
> —The Rev. William C. Graham

A bride writes: Our questions are about money. Should we give a gift to a family member who had already planned to attend the ceremony before we asked him to be a groomsman? How do we tactfully pay for out-of-town bridesmaids' hotels without getting stuck with their long-distance phone calls and room service? And finally, we want to pay the parking fees for only a few select guests (a large crowd is expected). Would it be in good taste to slip them a small envelope labeled "parking" with $5 inside? —PINCHING PENNIES

DEAR PINCHING PENNIES: Brides and grooms may be on a tight budget, but they should always have a reserve fund for those little incidentals that are "the gracious things to do."

Each person in the wedding party should receive a gift, no matter if he or she had already "planned to attend" before being asked to par-

 Tacky, Tacky, Tacky

Some couples don't even want gifts. They just want money. One couple decided to make it easy for their guests. They charged admission—$150 per person included dinner, dancing, and gift.

ticipate. Stiffing someone a gift is not the gracious thing to do. And if you are trying to save money on hotels, ask friends and relatives to host your out-of-town attendants.

Finally, no matter how generous you are trying to be, slipping someone $5 to pay for parking is insulting. If you want to pick up the tab for your guests' parking, arrange this beforehand with the parking garage.

A bride writes: It has always been an understanding in our family that the groom's family paid for the rehearsal dinner and the liquor tab at the reception, even though all the etiquette books say the bride's family pays for the reception. For my wedding, my parents are having a large reception and want my fiancé's family to pay for the liquor, about $1,500 to $1,700. My fiancé's family says that they have never heard of such a thing and accused my family of being cheap. My father insists that we serve alcohol, and my fiancé agrees that his family was wrong to say they would pay and then back out, saying they never heard of this custom. —BAMBOOZLED BRIDE

DEAR BAMBOOZLED: Hmm, what other customs has your family made up lately? Traditionally, the family of the bride picks up *all* of the expenses of the reception because the mother and the father of the bride are the hosts of the party. It is considered rude to ask the family of the groom, even if they are wealthier, to help pay for the reception. The bride's family limits a reception to what they can afford, whether that's a sit-down dinner for two hundred or just an afternoon tea, unless the groom's family offers to help.

However, it is inexcusably rude if the groom's family *offered* to help and then tried to back out. What you and your family must consider is that you will be dealing with these people long (we hope) after the bar bill has been paid in full. You may have to ask your family to be gracious about the "misunderstanding" for the sake of matrimonial harmony.

A bride writes: My fiancé and I are well established and have been living together. We don't need toasters and things. Is it appropriate to have a "wishing well" at the reception for gifts of cash and checks? —SEEING DOLLAR SIGNS

DEAR SEEING: Not by me. It is never correct to advertise blatantly for money gifts. In the South, gifts of money generally are sent before the wedding, but in some parts of the country, cash and checks are pressed discretely upon the bride, her father, or the groom during the reception. In many communities, the bride carries a silk purse for the gifts. But don't try this unless it is a part of your heritage.

A bride writes: Both my fiancé and I have been married before. I am thirty-six and he is forty-nine, and we are both well established in our careers and have complete households. We are planning a semiformal evening wedding. Is it bad etiquette to request a "money tree" on our wedding invitation or the response card? We certainly do not mean to offend anyone, but we don't need china, silver, or toasters! Would it be wrong to accept money to purchase something we really need? —GREEN THUMB

DEAR THUMB: Why don't you just print an admission price on the wedding invitation and sell tickets at the door? That's basically what you are suggesting. In your case, it is especially tacky because you have been married before and guests are not obligated to give you another wedding gift.

We all know that gifts are part of getting married, but the delightful pretense is that gifts are a happy by-product of weddings. Your friends want to show you their good wishes by commemorating the day. You as a bride must go along with that, or be thought horribly crass and crude.

On the other hand, thoughtful friends and family—the people who know and love you, the only people who should be invited to your wedding—will know that you don't need any more toasters. They will ask you what you need. *Then* you can tell them.

A bride writes: Is it improper or rude to have a cash bar at a wedding reception? The cash bar would be for beer, wine, and liquor. Champagne, punch, and soft drinks will be sponsored by my parents. Alcoholic drinks are extremely expensive, and since my parents don't drink for religious reasons, I don't think it is fair to make them bear that cost. —BAR MAID

DEAR MAID: When you invite people to a party—unless it's a charity event—you don't charge them admission, and a wedding reception is not a charity. It is a social occasion where one entertains one's guests.

As hosts, your parents are responsible for supplying food and drink. However, as hosts, your parents also have the privilege of planning the menu. If they don't wish to serve alcoholic drinks—whatever their reasons—then they shouldn't.

A bride writes: My fiancé and I are planning to be married on January 1 with a theme of "With This New Year, We Begin a New Life Together." His mother says being married right after Christmas will cut our gift receipts by one-third. I don't doubt that she is right. However, I really don't think that is her decision. What should I say to her? —GAGA OVER GIFTS

DEAR GAGA: What is this, a stage play? Couples don't need a theme for their weddings. A wedding is a ceremony of life.

When your "gift count" determines your wedding date, the reason for holding a wedding—to be surrounded by the love and support of family and friends as you begin your lives together—is getting lost. And I thought two people married because they were overjoyed to be spending the rest of their lives together, *not* to see how many presents they could get. I'm so speechless over scheduling wedding at optimum gift-getting times that I wouldn't know what to say to your fiancé's mother either.

A bride writes: When my sister married, she received many nice gifts but also many unneeded ones. One could claim that some of the guests did not check the bridal registry, but the truth is that many of them did not know where she was registered and did not call to find out. My fiancé and I are getting married next year, and we are planning a large wedding. I may be facing the same problem as my sister. Is it proper for a card with the location of the bridal registry to be included with the invitation? —REGISTERED BRIDE

DEAR BRIDE: Forgive me if I'm presumptuous, but are you one of those brides who has not only registered her china and silver patterns, but also which trash cans she prefers to get? It is never proper to ask for gifts, which is what you will be doing, no matter how you try to disguise it as convenience. Your guests took the time and trouble to select gifts they thought you would like; the least you can do is return them with a minimum of complaint about the bother of it all. If you proceed with your plan, you won't have to worry about having many gifts at all, much less some to return.

A bride writes: I am planning a wedding reception for approximately 250 guests. The catering company will charge me $15 per guest. Because of this, we are planning an adults only reception. I thought of enclosing a brief note along with the invitation to explain the situation. Here is an example:

∞

Dear Guests,
Please note that the reception is adults only. Due to economical reasons, children are excluded since the catering company is charging a fee per person. We deeply regret this decision since we would love to have children share the celebration of this occasion. We hope you will understand our decision.
Sincerely,
The Bride and Groom

∞

Would this note be considered proper etiquette? —NO KIDDING AROUND

DEAR NO KIDDING: No. The way to avoid having children at your reception is to not invite them. Do not put their names on the invitations. Do not have "adults only" engraved on your wedding invitations.

Ward off any parents who show up with tots in tow by providing a nursery. Your ushers can deflect any wayward mamas and daddies by directing them to the nursery.

For your information, all catering companies charge "by the head." If you sincerely want to have children attend the reception, try negotiating with your caterer to feed any wee ones at a discount.

A bride writes: My fiancé and I are having a hard time choosing our wedding party. He is the oldest of five. He has asked his brothers to be groomsmen, and he thinks I should ask his sister to be a bridesmaid. I am not close to his sister, and neither is he. I do not wish for her to be part of the wedding party at all. But he thinks that not only will people talk, but his parents will get mad and not come to our wedding. I always thought that you should ask the people you have a special relationship or friendship with to be in your wedding, not ask someone just because you had to! —NO SISTERLY LOVE

DEAR LOVE: Welcome to the real world, where grownups often have to do things they aren't keen on.

A bride does have the right to make decisions about her wedding, but her decisions should not be based on doing what she wants, acting as if she is queen for a day. If she wants to act like a monarch, then let her be a benevolent one. Her decisions must consider other people's feelings.

Do the gracious thing and ask your fiancé's sister to be a bridesmaid. It is a beautiful gesture that costs you nothing. It avoids problems with your future in-laws, and who knows? You and she may become strong friends.

Besides, after the wedding, your fiancé's sister will be your relative, too. She is someone you will see periodically and will share family stresses with. Wouldn't you rather have her on your side?

A bride writes: I am planning a formal wedding, and the ceremony and reception will both be held in a catering hall. I would like to indicate "Black Tie Invited" on the invitation, but I have been told it is not appropriate to put it there. Instead "Black Tie Invited" belongs on the response card. I would like to follow the correct rules of etiquette. Where does "Black Tie Invited" belong?
—BY THE BOOK

DEAR BY: Nowhere. As far as I am concerned, "Black Tie Invited" is a recent trend in the wedding business that is not correct.

There once was a time when people knew how to dress, but the days of intuitively knowing the dress code are long gone. When today's bride wishes her guests to dress formally, she indicates "Black Tie" in the lower right-hand corner of the invitation. Let's get rid of that "Black Tie Invited." It sounds as if you are inviting a suit.

A bride writes: I am planning a formal evening wedding in the fall. My fiancé's sister, one of the five bridesmaids, says she is going to a tanning parlor before the wedding. I am very much against this. It will look unnatural for someone to have a deep tan at a fall wedding. My girls are wearing black and teal velvet dresses, and her artificial tan would look terrible in person as well as in the pictures. (She has bleached blonde hair and tans very dark.) My fiancé "kind of" agrees with me. I have mentioned this to her several times very nicely, but she does not take me seriously. I do not want to cause family problems, but I do feel I should be granted this one wish. —PALE AND PROUD OF IT

DEAR PALE: Are you sure you can live with that bleached hair? Maybe you should get her to change that, too.

Sorry. A bride has the right to dictate what "her girls" will wear, but she doesn't have authority over makeup, hair, or skin color. That's going too far.

Still, one would hope most young women would be more concerned about wrinkles from exposure to UV rays. Leathery skin makes one look so old and, well, tough. And we've heard terrible stories about bad sunburns that left women looking bright red before important occasions such as weddings.

A bride writes: My husband and I were married five years ago in a very informal "surprise" elopement. We did not have a wedding ceremony, reception, or register with a store for gifts. My husband and I are now ready to have our "wedding with all the trimmings." Now we can afford to do it exactly the way we want. What kind of invitation should we give people who recognize us as being married? Should we explain why we waited? Would people think this is too strange and weird to attend? What about people who want to give gifts? The point of the wedding is not to make people feel obligated to give gifts, but if they insist, should we be prepared by registering with stores? How do we emphasize that the intent of this ceremony is to declare our feelings once again in public and to bring family and friends together?

Our situation is basically the same as people who have lived together before getting married. Should we treat this as a second marriage or simply a delayed ceremony? It has always been my dream to wear a stark white wedding dress. Besides, I look dreadful in pastels. Is it still improper etiquette to wear white and a veil if you are not virginal? Is it considered bad taste to have a wedding on the day other than which you were married? Is it awkward to have one's father give you away when you have been married for five years? Since we've been married five years, do you think bachelor and bachelorette parties are out of the question? —DREAMING

> ∞ "My second marriage was heaven on earth. Everything about it was what we wanted. Not mothers or preachers or caterers or that pesky old sow, convention."
>
> —Donna Perez, San Francisco bride

DEAR DREAMING: Dream on. You are married. You can't go back. If you want to have a big party and wear a white dress, do it, but don't try to call it a wedding. Five years is too long to wait to have a wedding with all trimmings after a civil ceremony.

You are making a mockery of the commitment and love represented by a wedding. What you want is to be queen for the day, and it is in such poor taste that I have no advice other than don't.

Thank-You Notes

Expressions of Gratitude and Good Taste

Two simple words, *thank you*, can mean so much, especially when they come from the heart.

You will find yourself searching for clever new ways to make this phrase more meaningful as you write people who have given parties for you or who have sent you wedding gifts. For friends and family who have been extraordinarily generous by hosting a shower or a party, send flowers or a bottle of wine.

But what about the dozens and dozens of thank-you notes you and your fiancé must write? How can you keep the notes from sounding boring and repetitive? How can you make them fresh and heart-felt? Every wedding gift requires a written note, even if you expressed your thanks in person.

First of all, remember that while you may have written ten notes at one sitting, the recipient of your gratitude probably will see just one—unless your friends and relatives have the habit of sharing their mail.

Thank-you notes need not be long, just three or four sentences. They must be timely, preferably within two weeks of receiving a wedding gift. But the true secret of the perfect thank-you note is personalization. Mention the gift, for example, "Thank you for the adorable hand towels embroidered with frogs." Say what the gift means to you or how you two plan to use it. "Since we collect frogs, the towels were the perfect gift for us. We plan to hang them in our new green and white guest bathroom."

For the grand finale, end with a flourish. "We cannot wait for you to visit so you can see how wonderful the towels look." Depending upon how close you are to the recipient, sign off with "love" or "fondly" or "sincerely" or "yours truly."

The proper paper is a small fold-over note with the bride's monogram (her initials) on the front. If the groom writes notes, he should use paper with his own monogram. I would prefer that you not use notes with "Thank You" printed on the front, but those are better than nothing.

Remember, a written thank-you note is always appropriate and appreciated, even when one is not required. When a friend or relative does something very special for the two of you, such as host a party or a shower, their generosity should be reciprocated with flowers or some other nicety in addition to a note.

Tacky, Tacky, Tacky

After her wedding, a South Carolina bride sent her guests generic fill-in-the-blank thank-you notes photocopied on small slips of paper. The guest's name and gift were neatly written on the blank lines. "At least she sent thank-you notes," said a bemused guest.

Here are some examples of thank-you notes:

FOR A WEDDING GIFT

Dear Betsey and Charlie,
David and I love the silver candlesticks you sent us as a wedding present.
They have a place of honor on our dining room table, and we will think of
you each time we dine by candlelight. We want you to be the first to share a
meal with us—by candlelight, of course—so I will be in touch when we get
back from our honeymoon.

> *With many thanks,*
> *Carole*

ॐ

Dear Mr. and Mrs. Jeffords,
Thank you so much for the lovely picture frame you sent. David and I agree
that it is perfect for a photograph of one of our favorite wedding memories, our
first dance together. Whenever we look at it, we will think of you. Thank you
so much for your thoughtfulness.

> *Fondly,*
> *Carole*

ॐ

FOR HOSTING A PARTY

Dear Lisa and Mike,
David and I hope you will enjoy these flowers as a small token of our
appreciation for your incredible generosity last night. We cannot thank you
enough for the fabulous cocktail party you gave us. We know all of our friends
and family will treasure their memories of the evening as we do, especially the

delightful toast Adam made. I don't think there was a dry eye in the house.
When we return from our wedding trip, you must come to dinner.

With many thanks,
Carole

∞

For Hosting a Shower

Dear Amanda,
You are the most wonderful friend. Not only do you put up with me
throughout all of this wedding planning, when I am sure I am driving you
crazy, but you also throw me a terrific shower. I cannot thank you enough, or
begin to tell you how much fun I had! I am so lucky to have you as a maid of
honor.

Thank you from the bottom of my heart!
Carole

∞

The Division of Labor

Since you're now officially a team, you and your new spouse agree that
you will share the job of writing thank-you notes for wedding gifts.
The best way to decide who writes to whom is for each of you to write
to people on your side of the guest list.

But let's face it. Guys are not trained from childhood to take pen
in hand and wax poetic over a pair of candlesticks while women, on
the other hand, can dash off several dozen notes without breathing
hard. Brides, you don't want to be a nag, but those notes have to be
written. After all, you are the kind of woman who cannot stand to

accumulate tacky penalties. Here are some tips to get you and your partner's creative juices flowing and get the job done:

• **Make it convenient.** Organize your materials in a basket or box so that paper, pen, stamps, and lists of addresses and gifts are in one spot. Make a habit of writing notes while you are watching television together or spend thirty minutes after dinner. (For more information on organizing a record of your wedding gift, please see Gifts.)

• **Make it easy.** Write out several examples of notes or use the ones above that he can copy. Remember to personalize each note, but keep it short. You don't need to write a book.

• **Make it fun.** Challenge each other to see who can write the most or the cleverest note. Barter with each other. Offer a reward of a kiss or a back rub or some other mutually-agreed-upon "gift" for every thank-you note produced. Soon you'll both look forward to taking pen in hand.

"BUT WE HATE IT!"

Writing thank-you notes for gifts you love is a piece of cake compared to trying to sound sincere when a wedding present is 1) awful and/or 2) unreturnable. Here are some ideas to get you started.

Dear Aunt Nell,

When Brad told me you were an artist, I had no idea. And then for you to give us one of your paintings, well, it's just overwhelming. Whenever we look at "Rainy Night," we will think of your generosity. Thank you for your thoughtfulness.

Fondly,

Janet

∞

Dear Melissa and Wally,

Brad and I were so pleased to receive the gold-plated salad tongs emblazoned with dice. Only you two could have come up with such an unusual gift, one that will always remind us of you. Thank you so much for your thoughtfulness, and we hope we will see you soon.

From the bottom of my heart,
Janet

∞

"Oops! Now What Do We Do?"

Certain situations call for a bride and groom to have the skill and tact of a diplomat.

• **You already have a toaster or whatever.** When you receive duplicates, thank both givers graciously. Then, if possible, exchange one of the dupes for something you need or for store credit. If the item cannot be returned, put it away with the idea of "recycling" it as a gift to someone else. You need not reveal your little deception to anyone.

• **The gift arrived broken.** Return it to the store for another one or a store credit. Retailers usually are happy to comply.

Tacky, Tacky, Tacky

Don't sign thank-you notes "Pat and Luanne" when only one of you did the writing. Instead, use your partner's name somewhere in the body of the note to convey that he or she also is grateful for the gift.

Tacky Penalties

Etiquette allows you a grace period for correspondence, but after that, tacky penalties accrue.

- You should answer invitations the next day.
- You have two weeks to write a thank-you note.
- You have a year to send a wedding gift.

"Oops! We Forgot to Say Thanks!"

No matter how organized you are, you may overlook someone accidentally and not send a note. When you discover your mistake, call the giver immediately and explain the oversight. True friends will forgive and forget.

The Unity Candle

"Now We Are One"

*U*nity candles symbolize the joining of two families. A divorce in the family does not preclude the couple from lighting a unity candle in hopes of a harmonious future.

Three candles, usually one large candle flanked by two smaller ones, are set on a table near the front of the room. The two side candles may be lit when the ushers light the other candles for the service, or the couple may ask their mothers to light the candles before taking their seats.

Then, at some point during the ceremony, the bride and the groom take the lit candles and together light the larger unity candle to symbolize their commitment to their marriage and the joining of their hearts. Your officiant can help you make this a part of your wedding service.

Wedding Myths

Believe It or Not

*B*rides and grooms get so much advice—most of it wrong—that they panic. It's like having a baby. As soon as people find out you're expecting a wedding, they feel free to tell you what to do, along with dire warnings about being improper (in other words, tacky).

The bride's mother is sure she knows what's correct. The groom's mother has her own ideas, and the neighbor down the street can't wait to talk about the horror stories she has from the tacky weddings she's attended. Then your stepmother weighs in with her suggestions. You begin to feel queasy at the thought of "your day."

Well, worry no more. Here are five wedding myths—and the right answers, no matter what anyone says. Folks will swear these myths are the eternal etiquette truths etched in stone and handed down by some great Etiquette God. They aren't, and you can quote me.

1. **The bride must be escorted down the aisle and given away by someone.** Being given away is a tradition that evolved from the days when men bought brides from their fathers or, even worse, captured them.

Today many young women feel this custom is archaic. Somehow it was charming when a woman went from her father's home directly to her new husband's, but that's not true of most couples today. With so many women going to college, supporting themselves, and marrying later, being "given away" seems terribly out of date. If you don't want it, leave it out. Ask your officiant to delete it from the service.

And, if she chooses, the bride *may* walk down the aisle by herself. Not every bride has a father; not every bride *likes* her father.

2. **The bride's father must sit in the first row with the bride's mother, even if they hate the sight of each other.** In a perfect world, divorced mothers and fathers would overcome their loathing so all can be sweetness and light on their child's wedding day.

Let's get real. Divorce is a fact of life. When divorced parents get along, it's wonderful. It's great. Mom and Dad can sit together, one big happy parental unit on the first pew.

This changes if stepparents are in the picture. Mom—and her new husband—should sit in the first row. Dad—and his new wife—should sit in the next row. If they do not get along, Dad and his new wife should sit even farther back—far enough away to avoid bodily harm. (All of this goes for the groom's parents, too.)

3. **The number of groomsmen must equal the number of bridesmaids.** So who's counting?! Unlike many other areas of modern life, there is no rule that says a wedding party must have equality. An equal number of men and women makes a pretty picture at the front—and makes life easier for the wedding consultant—but this is not mandatory. You can have all men, all women—even all children if you like. You don't have to be politically correct at your wedding.

4. **The flower girl and ring bearer must be under age six.** The younger kids are, the cuter they are—and the more they can disrupt your ceremony!

Flower girls have refused to go down the aisle or toss their petals. One little ring bearer grabbed the flower girl's basket, dumped the petals in a pile, and began jumping on them

The only criterion for the job of flower girl or ring bearer should be how important a child is to you. If the little girl or the little boy is someone you want to include, by all means do it, no matter how old— or young—they are.

5. **The bride's family has to foot all the wedding bills.** Once upon a time, the bride's father had that dubious honor, but life is no longer a fairy tale. Weddings are so expensive that often the groom's family offers to share the costs.

The operative word is *offers*. One commandment in the etiquette bible is there shall be no dunning of the groom's parents. They may offer to pay for the flowers, for instance, or for the liquor, but you can't force them. It's tacky.

Wedding Programs

A Wedding Who's Who

*W*edding programs help guests keep track of who's who, which is particularly helpful when the bride's and groom's families are blended and/or extended. Programs also are helpful in large weddings, when many of the guests may not know the couple well.

The program is usually a simple folded booklet much like a Sunday service bulletin that lists the order of the service and the music as well as the wedding party. The cover usually has the couple's names, the date and place of the wedding, and perhaps a decorative or liturgical motif.

Couples often use programs to explain the symbolism in the service or any unusual traditions that they have included. The program is also a place for the bride and groom to thank their parents and their guests for their love and support.

A bride writes: How do you organize the wedding program? I have a special poem my fiancé once wrote me, and I would like to include it in the program. Where and how would I include this? —MARRYING A ROMANTIC

DEAR MARRYING: What a lovely idea—as long as the poem doesn't have any X-rated stanzas! Many times couples are a source of great amusement to guests who find themselves stifling their laughter over poems and songs that mention making love or lying together in some fashion that just won't do for a wedding ceremony.

So, if your poem is G-rated, by all means include it in the program. Why not put it on the front, along with your names and the date of your wedding? The printer who is producing the program for you should be able to help with the design.

A bride writes: Both my fiancé and I have parents and grandparents who have remarried. I am very close to my stepmother and step-grandmother, as well as my half-brother and sister. We don't even refer to each other as "step" or "half." My fiancé, on the other hand, is close to his stepfather but not his stepmother. How do we write our program to acknowledge our families without using "step" or without leaving someone out? —PARENT TRAPPED

DEAR TRAPPED: Easy. If his name is Paul James MacKenzie, simply list his parents under the appropriate heading, for example, "Parents of the Groom: Mr. and Mrs. John Winkler Upjohn and Mr. and Mrs. Paul Benton MacKenzie." Do the same for your family. It's obvious who's who.

As for siblings, I would merely list their names under the heading, "Bridesmaids" or "Groomsmen." You don't have to spell everything out. This is a wedding program, not a family tree.

Weddings Away from Home

"Let's Run Away and Get Married"

A saying in my family, "been there, done that," applies as well to many couples today. For many men and women who have been married before, the thought of yet another trip down the aisle just isn't that exciting. It's déjà vu all over again.

When these couples recall their first wedding, everything was a blur of stress and tension as they married in a church that held hundreds of their parents' closest friends and business acquaintances, people they barely knew. This time, they vow, will be the wedding of their dreams, not their parents'. Often known as a "destination wedding," this wedding may be held on an empty beach on some Caribbean island. Or perhaps the couple weds on top of their favorite mountain, in a quaint European town, or in the garden of a beloved Victorian bed-and-breakfast.

Couples marry on the Battery in Charleston, on the beach in Jamaica, at Disney World, at Tavern-on-the-Green in New York, on the island of Nantucket, in a California vineyard, in the churchyard on St. Simons Island, or in Jackson Hole, Wyoming. Wherever their mood—and hearts—take them.

These wedding are usually tiny, just the couple, their parents, their children, and a few intimate friends. Everyone arrives a few days early to rest and relax, then the big moment. Then they all enjoy another day of relaxation on their built-in honeymoon. Everything is very casual, very personal, very *them*.

And when they come home, the couple invites their friends and relatives—as many as they can afford or want—to join them in an elegant party to celebrate their union. This party has all the trappings of a reception held just after a wedding ceremony: the cake, the receiving line, the music, the dancing, the photographs, the guest book, the decorations. But this party is different. It truly expresses the personalities of the bride and groom.

INVITATIONS

A couple who marries in this manner usually spreads the news of their marriage with wedding announcements mailed the day of the ceremony. (Please see Invitations and Announcements for wording.) The couple then follows this announcement with a party invitation mailed later, after they are home.

A reception held immediately after a wedding ceremony is a true "wedding reception," so a reception held several weeks later is more properly described as a party or as a "reception to honor Mr. and Mrs. John Q. Newlywed." The invitations are usually issued by the bride and groom. (Please see Invitations and Announcements for wording.)

"What Do We Wear?"

Many brides who choose to marry away from home don't want to spend hundreds of dollars on a gown they know they will never wear again. They already have that, packed up in a box for a daughter to wear someday. This time, they want a sophisticated suit or gown that looks wonderful and can be enjoyed again at their receptions when they come home. Still others opt for traditional gowns. Whatever the style, brides should feel free to wear their outfits again at their receptions.

A bride writes: Since this will be the second wedding for both of us, my fiancé and I would like to be married at a resort on Jamaica. The only problem is, we cannot afford to pick up the expenses for the few people we would like to invite. We can pay for our children, but no one else. Should we send these people invitations but tell them we cannot afford to pay for them? We want them to know we would have liked for them to be there, but we don't think they can afford the trip. —Beach Bride

Dear Beach Bride: How do you know these folks can't afford it? If these are friends and family you really want to include, by all means invite them. Let the decision be theirs when it comes to their pocketbook. You may be surprised.

 Here We Come!

One couple from Virginia was married on St. Barts, then invited friends and family to a formal party in a Richmond hotel. About half an hour into the party, the bride and groom disappeared. Then the lights dimmed and a video rolled of their wedding ceremony. As the video ended, the lights came up, revealing the couple in their wedding finery.

Instead of sending formal invitations, write letters to the folks you wish to invite. Tell them that you and your fiancé plan to be married at the Wedding Bells Resort in a casual ceremony on the beach on such-and-such date and that you would love for them to be there. Give the dates of your stay. In your note, mention your regret that you cannot play host to everyone, but that the resort is offering a discount. Give your guests the number to call to make reservations. Who knows? Perhaps your friends and family have been dreaming of a resort vacation for years, and your invitation was just the impetus they needed to pack their bags.

Index